HD30.4 .T635 2010
Tobin, Daniel R., 1946-
Feeding your leadership
 pipeline

DATE DUE

PRINTED IN U.S.A.

Praise for *Feeding Your Leadership Pipeline*

"*Feeding Your Leadership Pipeline* is the most comprehensive, practical, and inviting book on the fundamentals of leadership development that I have had the pleasure of reading. Tobin has done a masterful job of compiling all the tools, plans, processes, and programs that every small and medium-sized business needs to develop its future talent. And, it's extremely easy to read and easy to use. It's an extraordinary achievement, and you don't have to look any further than *Feeding Your Leadership Pipeline* for all the expert advice you need to build the leadership muscle in your organization."

Jim Kouzes
Bestselling coauthor, *The Leadership Challenge*
Dean's Executive Professor of Leadership, Leavey School of Business, Santa Clara University

"Tobin offers pragmatic, tested, and insightful approaches and tools to create an effective leadership development program tailored to small and medium-sized enterprises where improved talent can quickly make a difference. His four components of LDP (education, experience, guidance, and reinforcement) are well thought through and come with specific worksheets for making them happen. Any leader, HR professional, or trainer would be well served to follow his advice."

Dave Ulrich
Professor, Ross School of Business, University of Michigan
Partner, The RBL Group

"Dan Tobin designed and developed a leadership development program at the company where I was HR director. Based on the model for leadership development presented in this book, the program was an overwhelming success and helped the company to prepare its next generation of leaders. Many of the participants continued on into larger leadership roles both within and outside the company."

Karen Kinsley
Vice President, Talent Management & Development
Thermo Fisher Scientific

"Here is another gift to the industry from a man who is not following the trends, but setting them. Tobin's book is targeted in scope and application and focuses on methods that will produce measurable results rather than just activity and good intentions. His model—grounded on doing a few things, and doing them well—will help you succeed in attracting and leveraging your leaders of the future."

Jim Kirkpatrick, PhD
Kirkpatrick Partners
Author, *Training on Trial*

"*Feeding Your Leadership Pipeline* is a very timely and highly practical book. Dan's pulls together his extensive leadership development experience into a concise, engaging, and extremely helpful how-to format. His examples, charts, sidebars, checklists, and writing style make this gem a rare book that's both entertaining and a highly useful reference manual."

Jim Clemmer
Practical leadership author, workshop/retreat leader, and consultant

"Tobin's model for a leadership development program can help the small to mid-sized company build its next generation of leaders without having to invest in a large leadership development staff. His book is full of practical advice that can help CEOs and their HR staffs meet the challenges of filling senior positions that will soon open up as the baby boomer generation begins to retire."

Stewart D. Friedman
Bestselling Author, *Total Leadership: Be a Better Leader, Have a Richer Life*

"Dan Tobin is spot on both in his assessment of the need to develop next-generation leaders and in his approach to keep the 'leadership pipeline' full of capable candidates."

Ken Shelton
Editor and publisher, *Leadership Excellence*

"For those companies struggling with how to fill their leadership pipeline—but not fortunate enough to be blessed with an existing system—this book gives practical, effective, and affordable ideas for how to get started on developing the next generation of leaders before a shortage of talent becomes a business calamity."

Randall S. Peterson
Professor of Organizational Behavior and Deputy Dean (Faculty)
London Business School

"Business people face the same question: Who's going to run this company when I'm gone? Finding and nurturing the right people today will turn them into the best leaders tomorrow. This book is for any business owner who wants to ensure that the next generation will take good care of his or her company."

Gene Marks
Author, *In God We Trust, Everyone Else Pays Cash: Simple Lessons From Smart Business People*

"Over the past 10 years, middle-market businesses have become the object of affection for hordes of suppliers, provoking much dissonance among those in need of services. Where to turn for authoritative counsel? If structuring and building your entire leadership team is what's on your mind, go no further than Dan Tobin's *Feeding Your Leadership Pipeline*. Not only will it keep you out of trouble, it will help you supercharge your company for the power and growth phase that awaits you."

Allan Cox
Author, *Your Inner CEO*

"With a practical, common-sense approach, Tobin provides you with a process to create your own customized Leadership Development Program; the tools to implement it immediately; a perspective for how to enrich the value to your organization; and advice to ensure its success. If your organization is searching for a means to address its impending leadership gap, Tobin has a ready-to-implement answer, with an implementable idea on every page. This is the most useable leadership development book of its kind."

Elaine Biech
Editor, *The ASTD Leadership Handbook*
Author, *Training for Dummies*

Feeding Your Leadership Pipeline

How to Develop the Next Generation of Leaders in Small to Mid-sized Companies

Daniel R. Tobin

Alexandria, Virginia

Berrett–Koehler Publishers, Inc.
San Francisco
a BK Business book

ASTD Press is an internationally renowned source of insightful and practical information on workplace learning and performance topics, including training basics, evaluation and return-on-investment, instructional systems development, e-learning, leadership, and career development. Visit us at www.astd.org.

Ordering information: Books published by ASTD Press can be purchased by visiting ASTD's Website at store.astd.org or by calling 800.628.2783 or 703.683.8100.

Library of Congress Control Number: 2009930560

ISBN-10: 1-56286-710-5
ISBN-13: 978-1-56286-710-2

ASTD Press Editorial Staff:
Director: Adam Chesler
Manager, ASTD Press: Jacqueline Edlund-Braun
Senior Associate Editor: Tora Estep
Senior Associate Editor: Justin Brusino
Associate Editor: Victoria DeVaux

Copyeditor: April Michelle Davis
Indexer: April Michelle Davis
Proofreader: Kris Patenaude
Interior Design and Production: Kathleen Schaner
Cover Design: Ana Ilieva Foreman
Cover Art: iStockphoto, Frank Ramspott

Printed by Sheridan Press, Chelsea, MI, www.sheridanbooks.com.

Contents

Introduction

The statistics are clear. As reported by Natasha Tiku in *Inc.* magazine, "Over the next two decades, 78 million baby boomers will turn 65, the traditional retirement age. That's going to create a talent shortage, particularly in industries such as health care, education, engineering, and financial services. In 2005, workers over 55 represented 16 percent of the work force; by 2020 that will rise to almost 25 percent."

This book is designed to help small to mid-sized companies (defined as companies with fewer than 5,000 employees) that are struggling with the pending retirement of many of their leaders over the next five to 10 years and trying to determine from where their next generation of leaders will come. At one mid-sized utility, the general manager of power generation (the largest group within the company) said that nine of the 11 top people in his business unit were eligible to retire in the next five years and he had no idea where to find their replacements. When asked what the company had done to develop replacements for these key people, he replied: "I sent one guy to a weeklong program at [a well-known training vendor]. It cost a small fortune, and it didn't change a thing!"

Many large companies have built substantial leadership development organizations, usually as part of their human resources (HR) groups, to develop leaders at all levels of the company. Perhaps the most respected company in this category is General Electric, which has a long tradition of leadership development, consistently promoting new CEOs from within and supplying both themselves and many other *Fortune* 500 companies with generations of chief executives and other top-level officers.

In much of the business literature on developing future leaders within a business, General Electric's approach to leadership development is cited as a *best practice.* But few small to mid-sized companies have the resources to build a facility like GE's Crotonville, and most companies do not have large staffs dedicated to developing their companies' next leaders, so, for them, this best practice is irrelevant. The focus of this book is not on best practices, which may be only marginally relevant to the small to mid-sized company, but on *excellent practices* from many companies, large and small, and on approaches to help companies of all sizes develop their next generation of leaders.

It is these smaller companies, companies that are trying to determine how to grow their next generation of leaders without breaking the bank, that are the intended audience for this book. Whether you are the company CEO, head of HR, or training director, you will find many ideas for developing leaders within your company in this book. For leadership development professionals in larger companies, much of what you will read in this book may seem fairly elementary, but you may also find some new ideas here that can help you improve your current leadership development efforts.

LDP for a Mid-Sized Company

Some years ago, I worked for the senior vice president of HR at a small (1,500 employees) technology company. When I had interviewed for the job, I was told that one of my major responsibilities would be to design and run a leadership development program (LDP) for high-potential middle managers. During my first week, I asked my boss how he wanted me to start on the LDP. "It's not the right time now," he said. "Here's what I want you to start on now, and we'll get to leadership development at a later time." For my first 18 months, every time I asked about the LDP, I was told that "it isn't the right time."

Late one Thursday afternoon, I was called to my boss's office. "Now is the time. We have to do something about leadership development. Put together a design and a plan, and then let's review it." I was back in his office at 10 a.m. the following morning with the design and the plan. He quickly scanned it and said, "This is terrific! How did you get it done so fast?"

I told him that I had been working on it for 15 years. During this time, I had been collecting excellent practices from many companies around the world, both as part of my consulting work and research for my previous books on corporate learning strategies—all of those ideas had coalesced into this program design.

To make a long story short, I built and ran the company's LDP for 36 mid-level managers who had been identified by business unit heads and their HR partners as having high potential for future leadership positions in the company. The model provided for formal education sessions once a quarter, action-learning project assignments between sessions, 360-degree assessments, and individual development plans (IDPs) for each participant, and mentoring and coaching for some of the participants. The program was a great success, and many of the participants went on to higher-level positions both within the company and in other companies. The program also proved to be a great retention tool for these top performers: Of the 36 employees who had started the program, 35 stayed with the company through its completion.

In this book, an LDP model is presented. The model is designed for small to mid-sized companies that are concerned with developing their next generation of leaders.

Organization of This Book

Before designing an LDP, you need to define your target audience. Who among your current employees has high potential for future leadership positions? Chapter 1 deals with identifying high-potential talent and provides guidelines for identifying and screening candidates for the program.

Chapter 2 presents the four basic components of the LDP model:

1. education sessions
2. experiential and action learning
3. IDPs and guidance
4. mentoring, coaching, and reinforcement.

Chapter 2 shows how the components fit together to take participants through the four stages of learning, from being inundated with a plethora of unconnected data to developing the wisdom that will guide these participants as they are promoted to higher-level leadership positions.

Chapter 3 deals with the LDP education sessions—how to select topics, structure the sessions, and identify faculty to teach the sessions.

The action-learning projects that follow each education session are a key feature of the model and are detailed in chapter 4. Through these projects, LDP participants immediately start using what they have learned in the education sessions, which greatly helps with learning retention. These projects also yield other benefits, enabling the company to get some fresh thinking on some long-standing challenges and allowing company executives to observe the leadership behaviors of the participants.

Chapter 5 discusses the use of a 360-degree assessment for each participant along with other assessments that may be used in the formal education sessions. No matter how good your LDP education sessions may be, each participant will have unique development needs that may not be covered by your LDP agenda. Therefore, each LDP participant also needs to have an IDP.

Chapter 6 deals with setting up a mentoring program for LDP participants and arranging coaching as needed to fulfill the IDPs. Also of great importance in this chapter is advice on how to reinforce learning on the job to help ensure learning retention and to help participants apply their learning to their current jobs.

Assessment of the LDP participants and the overall evaluation of the LDP are discussed in chapter 7. In this chapter, you will learn about the concept of a learning contract that ties all learning to specific business goals and strategies and ensures that learning is applied to the job to make a positive difference in individual, team, and company business results.

For your LDP to be successful, many people and groups within your company will need to get involved. Chapter 8 discusses the various roles in planning and executing your LDP, including the role of an LDP manager.

Chapter 9 deals with how to get the program started and also how to conclude it. This chapter offers many bits of advice on designing and running this type of program.

Finally, chapter 10 reviews costs. When you first raise the idea of instituting an LDP in your company, one of the first questions that you will probably be asked is, "What will it cost?" You can find the answers here, along with many ideas for higher-cost and lower-cost options.

The book also includes an appendix in which there are brief outlines of a dozen education topics that you might consider for your LDP education sessions along with some ideas for the action-learning projects that might follow each.

It is my hope that this book will provide guidance to the thousands of small to mid-sized companies that are rising to the challenge of developing their next generation of leaders. As you read the book, please feel free to contact me at danieltobin@att.net with any questions or comments.

Chapter 1

Identifying Your Company's High-Potential Talent

What's In This Chapter

- What leadership competencies are most important for your company?
- How are key indicators of leadership potential identified and used?
- How are talent review meetings conducted and the results shared?

The small to mid-sized company typically does not have a leadership development staff to focus on succession planning and leadership development. Therefore, these responsibilities fall to the human resources (HR) staff, working in conjunction with the company's business leaders. Before you start planning a leadership development program (LDP) for your company's high-potentials (Hi-Pos), decide how you will identify those employees who will be placed in this group. While the selection will have subjective elements, a set of objective criteria must be developed by the company's HR staff, working with senior executives, to select those who will be designated as having high potential for future leadership roles. This chapter will discuss how to select those competencies that are most important for leaders in your company, how to determine which employees have the greatest potential for future leadership positions, how to create your pool of Hi-Pos, and how to complete the talent reviews.

The Numbers Don't Matter

It was the training director's first day on the job. Her boss, the senior vice president of HR, called her into his office and gave her assignment number one. Handing her a copy of a 360-degree instrument, he provided some background information along with the assignment.

"I've been trying for two years to get the CEO to approve our conducting 360-degree reviews of the top 150 employees. He keeps raising objections and offering new ideas. Go meet with him. Figure out what's bothering him about the process, and get it settled so we can get this started."

Later in the day, the meeting with the CEO took place. The CEO was a former engineering professor who had taken some of his university-based research, created the company 20 years earlier, and led it ever since.

"Have you seen all of the emails I sent on this?" asked the CEO.

"No, I haven't," replied the training director.

"Let me send you copies of the emails. Review them, and then we can meet tomorrow morning to discuss them."

The training director returned to her desk. The emails had already arrived—there were 28 of them, written over a period of two years. Each of them suggested adjustments to the score that would be generated by the 360-degree reviews:

- "If a person exceeded his goals by 10 percent, we should add 0.10 to his score; add 0.18 if the goals were exceeded by 50 percent."
- "If a person got a top rating on her last performance review, add 0.07; if the rating was above average, add 0.03 to the person's score."

The CEO was, after all, an engineering professor, and he wanted to come up with the perfect formula.

The next meeting took place the following morning.

"Did you read all of my emails?" asked the CEO.

"Yes, I did. And you made some very good points."

"So, you think we can come up with the perfect formula?"

"We can make many adjustments to the scores. But you need to realize one thing: the numbers don't matter," said the training director.

"What do you mean the numbers don't matter?!" The CEO was getting excited—he was a man who lived by numbers and formulas.

"Let's say that we come up with the perfect formula. After we do all of the 360-degree reviews and make all of the necessary adjustments to the scores, we have a rank-ordered list of the company's top 150 employees. And let's say that the top-ranked employee has an adjusted score of 4.34 and number two on the list has an adjusted score of 4.27. Tomorrow, for whatever reason, one of your direct reports leaves the company. Are you going to look at the list and say, 'The top score is 4.34; that person gets the job'?"

"Of course not! There is a lot more that has to go into that type of decision."

"Of course, you're right. You need to look at the employees' backgrounds and experiences, their strengths and weaknesses, and how well they fit the requirements of the job."

"Yes, of course."

"The numbers don't matter. They will give you some indications of how well the person is doing and how well that person is rated by his or her boss, peers, and employees, but the decision cannot be made solely on the basis of the scores."

The light went on in the CEO's head. "Okay, go ahead and get the process started."

Key Leadership Competencies

Competence is the ability to do something well. Every employee in your company has some competencies that are fully developed and some that need further development. The key competencies for leaders in your company depend on its culture, its way of doing business, the roles leaders play at different levels and in different business units and functional areas of your company.

While it is possible to create a list of dozens, or even hundreds, of competencies, all of those competencies will generally fall into three major categories (as explained by Tobin and Pettingell, 2008):

1. knowing and managing yourself
2. knowing and managing others
3. knowing and managing the business.

Knowing and Managing Yourself

All employees at all levels must have some self-knowledge and some capability to manage themselves. The competencies in this category are included in exhibit 1-1. If an employee hasn't mastered these types of competencies and demonstrated self-knowledge and the ability to manage himself or herself, and therefore isn't doing particularly well as an individual contributor, it is unlikely that the employee will be considered to manage or lead others.

Knowing and Managing Others

Competencies in this category are not the sole province of managers. Because no employee works in total isolation, all employees must develop

---

Exhibit 1-1. American Management Association competencies for knowing and managing yourself.

- Emotional Intelligence / Self-Awareness
- Self-Confidence
- Self-Development
- Building Trust and Personal Accountability
- Resilience and Stress Tolerance
- Action Orientation
- Time Management
- Flexibility and Agility
- Critical and Analytical Thinking
- Creative Thinking

Reprinted by permission from *The AMA Guide to Management Development* by Daniel R. Tobin and Margaret S. Pettingell © 2008 AMACOM, a division of the American Management Association, New York. www.amanet.org.

---

the competencies that allow cooperative work to take place, while managers need additional competencies to manage the work of their employees. Competencies in this category are listed in exhibit 1-2.

Knowing and Managing the Business

All employees need some basic competencies in this category to get their work done. Competencies in this category are listed in exhibit 1-3. For all employees, these include problem solving, results orientation, customer focus, and organizational savvy. For managers, there are additional competencies needed in this category, including strategic planning, decision making, business and financial acumen, and managing and leading change. Also in this category are competencies that are specific to the systems and

---

Exhibit 1-2. American Management Association competencies for knowing and managing others.

- Oral Communication
- Written Communication
- Valuing Diversity
- Building Teams
- Networking
- Partnering
- Building Relationships
- Emotional Intelligence / Interpersonal Savvy
- Influencing
- Managing Conflict
- Managing People for Performance
- Clarifying Roles and Accountabilities
- Delegating
- Empowering Others
- Motivating Others
- Coaching
- Developing Top Talent

Reprinted by permission from *The AMA Guide to Management Development* by Daniel R. Tobin and Margaret S. Pettingell © 2008 AMACOM, a division of the American Management Association, New York. www.amanet.org.

Exhibit 1-3. American Management Association competencies for knowing and managing the business.

- Problem Solving
- Decision Making
- Managing and Leading Change
- Driving Innovation
- Customer Focus
- Resource Management
- Operational and Tactical Planning
- Results Orientation
- Quality Orientation
- Mastering Complexity
- Business and Financial Acumen
- Strategic Planning
- Strategic Thinking
- Global Perspective
- Organizational Savvy
- Organizational Design
- Human Resources Planning
- Monitoring the External Environment
- Core Functional / Technical Skills

Reprinted by permission from *The AMA Guide to Management Development* by Daniel R. Tobin and Margaret S. Pettingell ©2008 AMACOM, a division of the American Management Association, New York. www.amanet.org.

technologies that drive your business as well as the technical competencies needed for the job, whether the job is in engineering, marketing, finance, or some other functional area.

Of course, there are additional competencies expected of company leaders, such as the abilities to

- create a vision and communicate and sell that vision to employees and other constituencies
- define the company's values and culture and not just communicate them to employees, but also live them

- create a top-performing executive team and align the team with the leader's vision
- translate a vision into specific goals and strategies.

It is rare to find the complete set of competencies in all three categories in any high-potential mid-level manager—some will be present and strong, some will be present but need further development, and others must be developed. What you need to look for in your Hi-Pos are indicators of the ability to develop these competencies over time through education and developmental assignments.

Your Company's Leadership Competency Model

Often, when doing succession planning, a company will compile a list of competencies that describe the incumbent in a given position. For example, "Our current chief financial officer has been very successful, so let's look at the competencies that he has and uses in his work." While this is a good starting point, relying on a job description based solely on the competencies of the incumbent in any position can lead to a suboptimal profile for that person's successor. For example,

- Sometimes the incumbent has had a unique career path in the company that cannot be duplicated in a successor.
- The incumbent may have a force of personality that has made him successful in this role, including flaws in that personality that have been overlooked, but which you don't want to include in the profile for a successor.
- You also need to look at the requirements for the position *in the future.* What has worked for the incumbent may not be sufficient for a successor given the changing nature of the business, future technology requirements, the growing internationalization of the business, and so on.

Even if you were able to create the perfect competency model for a position in your company, it is unlikely that you would be able to find a perfect candidate who exactly fits that competency model. Most executive recruiters spend a great amount of time and effort compiling the job profile for the perfect candidate. At the same time, they recognize that it is almost impossible to find such a perfect candidate, so most headhunters and the companies for which they work will settle for one who has an 80 percent match to that ideal profile.

Focusing on Key Indicators of Potential

What are the key competencies that will sustain your company and help it grow in the future? In identifying employees who have high potential for future leadership positions in your company, determine what personal characteristics and competencies are the keys for your company. When you start out, it is unlikely that there will be a large pool of promotable employees immediately ready to step up to higher responsibilities. But you can identify a set of key indicators for those who should be put into the high-potential pool. Below are some ways to help make this determination:

- Besides doing work proficiently, have the employees shown interest in other parts of the business? Do the employees look beyond specified job responsibilities to better understand the business processes of which their work is a part? Do the employees work to just get the work done, or do the employees look for ways to optimize the larger business process?
- How well have the employees worked as part of a team? Have the employees stepped up to lead teams? How well have the employees supported other team members? When there was a tight deadline, were the employees willing to step in to help other team members?
- How good are the employees' ideas? Have the employees been able to find new and better, more efficient, or more effective work methods? Have the employees been able to solve their own problems, or are the employees totally dependent on their managers when something goes wrong? If the employees have worked on cross-functional teams, how impressed have people from other functions been with the employees' ideas and contributions?

Table 1-1 presents a basic framework you can use to identify Hi-Pos based on two dimensions: potential for future leadership positions and current job performance.

Table 1-1. Identifying high-potentials.

		Potential for Future Leadership Positions		
		Low	Medium	High
Current Job Performance	Low			Davis
	Medium	Berman		
	High	Schultz		Shelley

Here are some examples of how this type of categorization can be used with your employees:

- Berman is a steady performer. He gets his work done, but doesn't go beyond the job. He does the minimum to get the job done, participates in teams reluctantly, and generally doesn't make himself available to help co-workers. His current job performance is rated as medium, but his potential for future leadership roles is rated as low.
- Davis is recognized as very bright. She has had some great ideas but seems bored with her current job. She has the right background for the job but seems eager to do more. She impresses everyone with her ideas but isn't a doer. Her potential is rated as high, but her job performance is rated as low.
- Schultz always earns top ratings on her performance reviews. She is very efficient and always willing to put in the time and effort to get the job done. At the same time, she doesn't seem to have the intellectual capacity to move beyond her current job. She is a doer but not a strategic thinker. She doesn't display any real business acumen beyond her current position. Her job performance is rated as high, but her potential to grow into a future company leader is rated as low.

- Shelley is an exceptional performer, continuously earning top performance ratings. He also is a great team player, constantly helping others and bringing them along. He has great ideas and has made a number of improvements in work methods within his own department, as well as being a very productive member of several cross-functional teams. His ratings on both scales are high.

Compiling Information on High-Potentials

It takes more than a gut feeling to identify an employee who has high potential for future leadership positions in your company. Gut feelings, while sometimes correct, tend to be too subjective. Task your HR business partners for each business unit, functional area, and geographic area with compiling information on each candidate. This information should include the following:

- A copy of each person's résumé provides background information on the person's education and work experience. Too often, employees are defined by their current jobs. Their résumés can point out other areas of education and experience that may provide useful information when looking at the employees' future career paths.
- Copies of each person's last two or three performance reviews in the current job, as well as a history of the person's progression within the company, help you look beyond a single job rating. Are the employees' managers known as hard markers who rarely give high ratings or easy graders who give high ratings no matter how well or poorly the employees do their jobs?
- Anecdotal information about the employee's potential can come from anyone with whom the employee has worked, not just the employee's immediate manager. What have the employees done that make you believe that they may have high potential for future leadership positions? In some cases, employees may be given relatively low performance ratings because they work for managers who are not open to new ideas, while co-workers and others rightly value the employees' ideas.

Initial Ratings

The person who best knows each employee's work is that employee's direct manager, and that manager can do the initial ratings of performance and potential using a form developed by the HR staff. An example form is given in exhibit 1-4. But filling out a form isn't sufficient in and of itself, for not all of the manager's feelings about an employee can be, or should be, expressed in writing. Therefore, each manager can meet with a member of the HR staff to discuss the ratings. HR staff often have their own networks among employees and collect their own intelligence on employee performance and potential. While in the ideal world, HR and managers would be in perfect agreement, there are several common situations where HR's judgment may overrule a manager's ratings of an employee:

- In an international company, an employee's manager may reside in a different country from the employee and, therefore, have a limited line-of-sight regarding the employee's performance and potential. In such cases, the country HR manager may be able to provide a more informed opinion on these matters.
- Some managers may try to hoard good employees. That is, if an employee is doing a great job and could not easily be replaced, the manager may find it personally advantageous to give the employee a low rating on potential for fear that the employee will be promoted out of the group or otherwise be assigned elsewhere.
- Like it or not, there are some poor managers in almost every organization. A poor manager may not like a particularly bright employee who challenges the manager's judgment or tries to stretch beyond specific job responsibilities. In these cases, the manager may rate the employee poorly, even though the employee has the potential to be an outstanding performer or to grow beyond the current job.

Talent Review Meetings: Level I

After the preliminary work is done by managers and HR reps, the group managers should hold talent review meetings with the managers in their groups and their HR business partners to discuss the ratings and

Chapter 1

Exhibit 1-4. Rating of Employee Performance and Potential.

Employee Name: _____

Business Unit/Function: _____

Current Job Title: _____

Years in Job: _____ **Years in Company:**_____

Manager's Name:_____

Current Performance Rating: _____

Explanation of Current Rating:_____

Rating of employee's current potential (check one):

☐ Employee is not a good fit for current job—recommend dismissal

☐ Employee is not a good fit for current job—recommend finding another role

☐ Employee needs more time in current job to master it

☐ Employee does current job well, needs job enlargement

☐ Employee is ready for promotion to next level

Explanation of Rating:_____

Rating of employee's future potential (check one):

☐ Employee is at risk of losing current job and has no potential for the future

☐ Employee is good at current job but has little potential to grow beyond it

☐ Employee has good potential for advancement in a technical career track

☐ Employee has good potential for the next level of management

☐ Employee has good potential for growth to middle/senior management

☐ Employee has high potential for future company leadership roles

Explanation of Rating:_____

Manager's Recommendation (check one):

☐ Dismiss employee

☐ Develop employee in current job
  Explain: _____

☐ Provide additional training
  Explain: _____

☐ Look for new role for employee
  Explain: _____

☐ Promote employee
  Explain: _____

to determine who might be put into the high-potential pool. Additional insights may come from this group meeting. For example, someone in the group (other than the employee's direct manager) may have had an opportunity to see the employee work as part of a cross-functional team or may have heard comments about the employee from his or her own direct reports.

Group managers must make these talent review meetings a high priority for their teams, and the discussions in these meetings must be frank, open, and confidential. The outcomes of a talent review meeting may include the following decisions:

- to terminate some employees
- to assign greater responsibilities to some employees to see how well they perform with an enlarged job scope
- to send some employees for training
- to find new roles for some good employees who are not a good fit for their current job roles
- to promote some employees
- to designate some employees as having high potential for future leadership roles and to either put them in an LDP or have HR work with the employees and their managers to create individual development plans
- to recommend that some Hi-Pos be included in the company's executive talent review.

Talent Review Meetings: Level II

It is also vital for the organization's executive committee (CEO and direct reports) to hold an executive-level talent review at least once a year. Focus the talent review at this level on the top end of the leadership pipeline, that is, those employees who are, or will soon become, part of the leadership team's succession plans. Each member of the executive team, along with the respective HR business partner, can present a report on each of their top candidates, focusing on the following:

- For employees who previously have been reviewed, the executive committee member and the HR partner present progress made since the last review. For example, if the employee had been given a new developmental assignment, how well did the employee do in that role? If the employee had been sent for some training, what were the results (in terms of job performance)?

- For employees new to the executive talent review, the executive committee member and the HR partner present a broad overview of the employee including educational background, job history, notable achievements, strengths and areas needing development, and reasons why the employee has the potential for future leadership roles in the company. The executive committee member and the HR partner can also make recommendations on the next steps in the employee's development.

- If the company has initiated an LDP and the executive team has participated in the program (as described in chapters 7 and 8), executives may also bring into the talent review discussion any participants in that program who they believe are showing high potential for the future. The committee members can also discuss the types of topics and action-learning projects they want to recommend for the next rounds of the LDP. (Executive talent reviews for participants in the LDP are discussed at greater length in chapter 7.)

- It is also vital that the talent review includes all business units, all functional areas, and all geographies in which the company does business. In too many cases, because the members of the executive team tend to be co-located at company headquarters, their view of talent tends to be myopic—focusing on local talent and on who will lead the organization's major business units. It is equally important that the committee review talent in functional areas, such as information technology, finance and accounting, and HR, and that they look for talent wherever the company operates.

It is important that the executive committee make a real commitment to doing these talent reviews. They need to prepare for them, and they need to work closely with their HR business partners. They also need to first agree to take the time to do a proper job—if a talent review is done properly, this annual session may last for two or three days. Too often, executives pay lip service to doing this type of review and then never find enough time to do the job right. There is nothing on the executive agenda more important than ensuring that the organization prepares its future leaders. (For an excellent description of one company's executive talent reviews, see *Execution: The Discipline of Getting Things Done* by Larry Bossidy, Ram Charan, and Charles Burke, 2002.)

Results From the Talent Review Process

After the talent review process is completed (although it is in reality never finished but continued on a periodic basis), it is up to the HR group to compile the results:

- which employees will be terminated
- which employees will be assigned greater responsibilities to test their abilities or to give them exposure to other parts of the business
- which employees will be sent to internal or external trainings
- which employees will be reassigned to different jobs or promoted to a new position with greater responsibility
- which employees are to be designated as having high potential for future leadership positions and will be put into the company's LDP.

It is this last group of Hi-Pos and the LDP into which they will be placed that are the focus of the rest of this book.

Employees and Their High-Potential Designation

There is an ongoing debate as to whether employees who have been designated as Hi-Pos should be told of this designation, and there is no clear answer to the question. Table 1-2 summarizes the pros and cons of telling versus not telling.

The people who argue for telling employees of their designation as high potential feel that this can be a motivator and a retention tool. In one company, many of them said after the first or second session of the LDP

Table 1-2. Should employees be told about their high-potential designation?

	Tell Employees	Don't Tell Employees
Advantages	• Helps retain and more effectively engage employees • Allows each employee to make conscious career decisions • Inspires other employees to work for high-potential status	• Avoids ego problems • Doesn't engender jealousy among others • Makes it easier to later decide to remove employee from high-potential pool
Disadvantages	• Leads to ego problems • Leads Hi-Pos to think they have a free pass • Discourages employees who aren't designated • Discourages employees who are later removed from the pool	• Leads Hi-Pos to leaving for better opportunities elsewhere because they don't feel they are being recognized • Doesn't allow company's investment in talent to be made visible to employees

that they had been looking for employment outside the company. They also said, "If the company is going to make this investment in my future here, I'm going to stick around." And, in fact, they did stick around with 35 of the 36 staying the course for the entire two-year program. After another session in the LDP, where the seminar leader talked about "navigating in stormy seas" (which the company had been experiencing for several years), several participants said that they thought that they had been acting like navigators, but now realized that they were acting like victims (using the seminar leader's terminology) and that they were now ready to become more engaged in their work.

By making the high-potential designation public, and making visible the LDP for those Hi-Pos, there were some trickle-down effects. A number of employees who had not made the list asked why they hadn't been included and clearly stated (verbally and, even more important, behaviorally) that they were going to set a personal goal to be included on the next high-potential list and in the next LDP.

Those who argue against telling employees of their high-potential designation cite several possible disadvantages. Foremost among their objections is that employees who are told of their high-potential designation may develop overinflated egos and feel that they are being given a free ride to the executive suite. They also argue that the designation of a high-potential pool may discourage those who aren't placed into this pool, causing additional problems with retention, engagement, and jealousy.

To give LDP participants a dose of reality, employees told of their high-potential designation are often also told the following:

- The designation can be withdrawn at any time if the employees' behavior or quality of work in the LDP or on-the-job declines.
- They have a responsibility, as part of the LDP, to do additional work while continuing to do their current jobs. A general estimate was that the LDP would add 10 to 15 percent to their workload. (This may vary depending on the design of your LDP.)
- Designation as a Hi-Po in no way guarantees future promotions. Future promotions will be made on the basis of merit, achievement in the LDP, quality of work on the LDP's action-learning assignments, and availability of promotional opportunities.

Another important reason for letting employees know they have been identified as having high potential for future leadership positions is to give them a choice—not everyone wants to become a leader with all of the additional responsibilities. For example, after the first session of one LDP, one employee announced that he wanted to drop out of the program. He was gratified to have been chosen for the program, but he recognized the extra effort that would be required from him both for the program itself and for the higher-level positions to which he might aspire after the program. As he listened to a discussion of work–life balance issues in that first LDP session, he made a conscious decision that he was happy with his life in the position he now held and that he wanted to use whatever extra time he had to focus on the needs of his family. It was a good decision for him and, in the long run, for the company, because had he been promoted and found that the responsibilities of higher-level jobs were too much for him, he would probably have left the company. By making the decision early, he was happier and the company got to retain a valuable employee.

Management Ladder versus Technical Ladder

Many companies have created a technical ladder career path that parallels their management ladder career path. The purpose of a technical ladder is to provide promotional opportunities for employees who bring great value to the company through their technical expertise and want to focus their careers on that expertise rather than build their careers through entering and rising through the management ranks. These companies have created a career path for these technical employees with titles and rewards that parallel manager, director, and vice president ranks using such titles as "consulting engineer" or "corporate marketing consultant" in lieu of management titles such as "engineering director" or "vice president of marketing."

In most companies that use this approach, there are very specific criteria—a different set of competencies—that employees must meet to be promoted on the technical ladder. These criteria typically include the following:

- contributions to company products or services
- patents obtained
- reputations (external to the company) in their field of expertise
- presentations at industry conferences or technical papers for industry journals
- mentoring of junior technical staff.

Typically, employees who want to be promoted on a technical ladder must prepare a portfolio that documents their achievements, and that portfolio is reviewed by a panel of senior company officers who pass judgment on each application.

The people who run the technical ladder program often criticize the company's management ladder for not using a similar set of criteria in deciding on promotions to management positions—the establishment of your company's LDP, including the talent review process, will help counter these complaints.

While technical ladders were started primarily in technology companies, their scope is not limited to technological areas such as engineering or manufacturing, but are also used in fields such as marketing, sales, and finance.

In selecting Hi-Pos for an LDP, you should consider these two alternate career paths. Chapter 3 recommends that the first session of the LDP deal with a discussion of what leadership means and the requirements to become a leader in the company. As an action-plan follow-up to that first LDP session, LDP participants should write a personal vision statement—and this is the perfect place and time for the participants to choose whether they want technical ladder or management ladder career paths. (For more detailed information on technical career ladders, see Michael Badaway's *Developing Managerial Skills in Engineers and Scientists: Succeeding as a Technical Manager.*)

Summary

The LDP model presented in this book focuses on developing your company's next generation of leaders. The process starts with the identification of a group of Hi-Pos who will participate in this program. This chapter has covered how to identify your company's Hi-Pos through data collection and talent review processes that include company executives, managers, and HR partners.

The next chapter will examine the overall LDP model and how the various elements of the model fit together to help develop your company's next generation of leaders.

Chapter 2

Components of a Leadership Development Program

What's In This Chapter

- What are the four essential building blocks of an effective LDP?
- How do the four building blocks work together to cover all four stages of learning?
- What expectations should you set for the results from your LDP?

Small to mid-sized companies often struggle with building a consistent, replicable leadership development program, opting instead to send high-potentials to external trainings or let the cream rise to the top. This chapter presents a structured approach to building your company's LDP that is easy to build and duplicate over time. This chapter will also relate the LDP model to the four stages of learning to demonstrate the benefits of the model.

The LDP model has four basic components, as shown in figure 2-1:

1. education sessions
2. experiential and action learning
3. individual development plans and guidance
4. mentoring, coaching, and reinforcement.

While the LDP model includes all four of these components, depending on your company's needs and the resources available, you may choose to focus on one or more of the components or some combination of two or more components. In this chapter, the focus is on how all four components fit together into a comprehensive LDP. Chapters 3–6 will go into much greater detail on the content and variations for each component.

Before starting to examine each component of the LDP model, step back to consider why you are concerned with developing your company's next generation of leaders and what the goals of your LDP should be. The reason that companies invest in leadership development is to ensure that the company will have the talent it needs to do business and to grow both today and tomorrow. The LDP is designed to prepare the next generation of leaders by giving them the education and work experience they need to prepare for larger roles in leading and managing the company in the future. Some companies invest little in this process, assuming that the cream will rise to the top or that they can always hire the talent they need from the outside. More enlightened companies invest in the learning of their Hi-Pos to facilitate and accelerate their preparation for larger roles.

To better understand how the various segments of the LDP model fit together, first examine a basic model of how people sort through the

Figure 2-1. Leadership development program model.

Education Sessions		
Experiential and Action Learning	Individual Development Plans and Guidance	Mentoring, Coaching, and Reinforcement

vast array of data they see every day, select those pieces of data that become information, build knowledge from that information, and then develop wisdom.

Four Stages of Learning Model

The four stages of learning model can help you understand the LDP model and help you design an optimal LDP that will facilitate the participants' journeys through the four levels while focusing them on the needs of the company. Figure 2-2 shows the four stages of learning: data, information, knowledge, and wisdom.

Stage I: Data

Everyone is inundated by data—everything people take in through their senses is data—every email and website they read, every conversation they hold, everything they see and hear is data, and people are drowning in it. Some data is useful to people in their work—one of people's greatest challenges is how to separate the useful from the vast majority of data for which they have no use.

Stage II: Information

Peter Drucker (1993) said that when data is imbued with relevance and purpose, it becomes information. In designing your LDP, you want to make certain that what you are providing is *information* rather than just more data.

Figure 2-2. The four stages of learning.

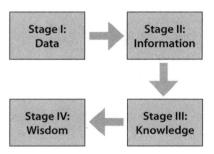

So, how do you ensure that the educational content of your LDP is relevant and purposeful? Here are three guideposts you can use:

- core leadership competencies
- leader priorities
- participant learning needs.

Core Leadership Competencies

Chapter 1 discussed how to identify your company's core leadership competencies to use as a guidepost in selecting Hi-Pos. These same competencies can be used to guide your selection of topics for inclusion in your LDP. Some of those competencies will already be present in your LDP audience (or they wouldn't have been selected as Hi-Pos to begin with), but others will stand out as areas for further development.

Leader Priorities

In too many companies, leaders complain the training/talent development/ leadership development group doesn't understand the company's business and that while the programs it offers are interesting, their value is limited because they rarely address pressing company needs. The best way to tie the LDP content to the needs of the company is to ask company leaders about their priorities:

- What current issues would you like the LDP to address?
- What sets of knowledge and skills do you see lacking in the company's next generation of leaders that can be addressed in the LDP?
- How can the LDP best ensure that your and the company's needs are addressed directly?

Asking these questions up front, before you plan any type of education session for the LDP, will ensure executive buy-in and support because executives will see that everything you are doing is targeted directly at those issues they consider most important. And by getting executive buy-in to the issues being addressed, you will also find it much easier to get the same executives to actively participate in the LDP. (Find more on executive roles in the LDP in chapter 8.)

Participant Learning Needs

There are two primary methods to assess the LDP participants' learning needs. The first is to ask them and their managers, because no one knows these needs better than they and the people who manage their work every day: What topics would you like to see included in the LDP education sessions? Also ask them why they have chosen each topic and to prioritize among the list of topics that they generate.

The second method is the third component of the LDP model, which includes a variety of assessments and the writing of an individual development plan (IDP) for each participant. For example, if you do a 360-degree review of each participant and then aggregate the findings across all participants, there are certain to be areas for development required for most or all of the LDP group. However, there will also be topics on which only one or a few participants need further development, and those should become part of the IDPs, rather than the overall LDP education agenda.

With this information, you can ensure that what the LDP provides is information, rather than data—that it has relevance to the company and to the participants and that there is a purpose for each topic that will be included in your learning agenda.

Stage III: Knowledge

Just learning *about* various topics isn't enough. You want to ensure that what is learned is actually used to make a positive difference in achieving individual, team, and company goals.

Knowledge comes from applying information to your work. For example, you can read a lot of material on how to ride a bicycle, watch instructional videos, and observe others riding their bicycles, and that is all good information—it has relevance (assuming you want to learn to ride) and it has purpose (to teach you to ride). But you cannot say that you *know how* to ride a bicycle until you do it yourself. This is the purpose of the experiential and action-learning components of the LDP model—to get participants to immediately apply what they have learned to help them turn the information from the education sessions into personal knowledge. Without this step, much of what was learned in the education sessions, no matter how excellent the instruction, would soon be forgotten.

They're All Very Smart

Some years ago, I met a senior managing partner at one of the world's largest accounting and consulting firms. He proudly told me that he was sponsoring a program that summer to send 3,000 of the firm's associates to two days of lectures by one of the best-known leadership gurus at a leading business school. They would be flown in to the sessions, in groups of 300 from all over the world, and would listen to the guru lecture for two days.

I asked him some questions about the program:

- How had they determined exactly what content the guru would include in the lectures to ensure that it aligned with the firm's goals? His answer: "This is one of the world's leading authorities on leadership. We wouldn't presume to tell him what to include in his lectures."

- How would the associates be prepared for the education sessions? His answer: "We're sending each of them a copy of [the guru's] latest book and telling them they should read it before the session."

- What would the associates be expected to do with what they learned? Was there a plan for following up on the lectures? His answer: "Our associates are very smart. They'll figure out what to do."

I knew this guru's work well, and it was excellent material on leadership. But without making a connection to the firm's business goals, without any real preparation or setting of expectations, and with no follow-up to the education sessions, I estimated that the firm was probably wasting a few million dollars.

Stage IV: Wisdom

Wisdom cannot be taught, but it can be developed through dialogue, demonstration, and reflection on experience. The development of wisdom through the LDP will come from three primary sources:

1. dialogue with company executives and subject matter experts, both in education sessions and through mentoring and coaching of participants
2. dialogue with fellow LDP participants and others
3. reflection on learning and experience through the debriefing of action-learning projects and keeping a personal learning journal.

Dialogue with Company Executives and Subject Matter Experts

As will be discussed in chapters 4, 6, and 8, there are vital roles for company executives to play in the LDP. On certain topics, they may act as faculty, but more important they can hold an ongoing dialogue with the LDP participants, by reflecting on their own personal leadership journeys and the lessons they have learned along the way, by educating the participants on the company's culture and values and exemplifying both through their own behaviors, and by sharpening the participants' critical thinking skills by reviewing and debriefing their action-learning projects. Outside the formal educational structure of the LDP, executives can also act as mentors, offering counsel on the participants' own leadership journeys and steeping their mentees in the company's and the industry's history.

Dialogue with Fellow LDP Participants and Others

More than half the value of the LDP will come not from formal education activities that you plan, but from the dialogue that participants hold among themselves. After a first meeting of an LDP group, it is not uncommon to hear participants comment: "You know, if there had been no education session, but the company had just paid for all of us to come together and talk with each other for a few days, it would have been worth the company's investment."

Along with these dialogues with other LDP participants, Hi-Pos may also interact with faculty, their coaches, their managers, and others as part of their action-learning projects and experiential-learning assignments and in the course of everyday business. These dialogues can help participants develop their own wisdom by exercising their critical and creative thinking skills.

Reflection on Learning and Experience

Leadership skills are not developed by rote. That is, developing leadership skills is not as easy as memorizing multiplication tables, because there is no one universal leadership model. Participants in the LDP must listen to the many approaches that will be presented through education sessions and figure out what will work for them and the company. This may require some experimentation and some adaptation of what they have learned so that the same educational theme may result in many variations on that theme, each personally tailored to the characteristics of the individual participant.

The use of the personal leadership journals, as will be explained in chapter 5, can help reinforce employees' learning and the development of their personal wisdom.

Components of the LDP Model

While each component will be discussed at length in its own chapter, the focus now is how the components will help participants work through the four stages of learning to help you create a comprehensive LDP that will indeed help you create your company's next generation of leaders (see table 2-1).

Table 2-1. Relating the four stages of learning to the LDP model.

Stages of Learning	LDP Model Components
Stage I (Data) ➡ Stage II (Information)	• Relevant content selection • Needs assessments
Stage II (Information) ➡ Stage III (Knowledge)	• Action-learning projects • Virtual follow-up sessions • Reinforcement
Stage III (Knowledge) ➡ Stage IV (Wisdom)	• Mentoring • Dialogue (debriefs) • Reflection (personal journals)

What results can you expect from your investment in the LDP? Here are some reasonable expectations:

- Through a comprehensive set of educational sessions focused on your company's key competencies, you will help participants develop the business acumen and execution skills they will need when they assume new leadership roles.
- You will expand and improve the quality of your company's bench strength and have a larger pool of qualified talent when developing the company's succession plans.
- You will retain some of your top talent that you might not otherwise have kept—employees who see that the company is investing in their future with the company are more likely to stay. For many employees who were not selected for the LDP, you will create an incentive to improve their performance so that they can qualify for the next group of LDP participants.
- Through action-learning projects, you will solve some long-standing company challenges that might otherwise never have been addressed.
- You will make visible to the company's executive team a wide range of talent that they might otherwise never have seen.
- You will see participants improve their performance in their current jobs as a result of what they learn in the LDP.
- You will be able to weed out some employees who had seemed to be rising stars, but who failed to perform well in the LDP, which will help the company avoid potentially costly promotional errors.
- You will help company executives feel more connected to many parts of the business through their participation in the LDP.

Education Sessions

Formal, classroom-based, instructor-led educational sessions are the core of the LDP model. Learning to be a leader is not a solo activity, and studying on one's own does not provide the opportunities for the dialogues that are so important to the development of individual leadership wisdom. While in today's pressure-packed business environment many people are reluctant (if not recalcitrant) to take time from their daily jobs to attend a formal education session, consider requiring that your group of Hi-Pos make this investment in their own future, even if it adds to their regular workload. Further, for the younger generations who are so reliant on instant everything (text and email messages, Twitter, and others), the social aspects of learning together with others, without constant interruptions, and establishing face-to-face dialogues are important lessons to be learned.

But attending an education session or a series of sessions, even though you have selected education topics that are relevant to the audience and have purpose for them (moving them from Stage I to Stage II of the learning model), isn't enough to ensure the development of knowledge. The real power of the LDP model is that every educational session is followed by a subject-matter-related action-learning project.

Experiential and Action Learning

Action-learning projects help participants transform information reaped from the education sessions into personal knowledge, moving them from Stage II to Stage III of the learning model.

As will be explained in chapter 4, each action-learning project, whether completed individually or as a team, needs to be based on the lessons learned in the classroom and the application of those lessons to real challenges facing the company. And, as a bonus, as participants work on their action-learning projects, they will also be developing their teamwork and team leadership skills, learning about other parts of the business that had not necessarily been in their lines of sight, and developing their business acumen as they learn more about the company's business processes.

Educational sessions are aimed at a common denominator—those topics that are most vital to *all* future company leaders and those designed to help overcome knowledge and skill deficiencies across the entire high-potential group. But each participant will be different and may have specific personal learning needs as discovered through a 360-degree review and other assessment instruments.

Individual Development Plans and Guidance

The third component of the LDP model calls for IDPs and guidance for each participant. While it is recommended that all participants undergo a 360-degree review, there will also be other assessment instruments used as part of the formal education sessions that can point to areas of development for each individual that may differ from those of the overall group.

It is therefore recommended that the company's HR group take responsibility to work with each participant and the participant's manager and mentor to tailor an IDP to complement and supplement the LDP. These plans are discussed in greater detail in chapter 5.

While all of these model components will lead to learning, it is also important that learning be reinforced through mentoring, coaching, and other forms of reinforcement.

Mentoring, Coaching, and Reinforcement

Mentoring, coaching, and reinforcement are vital considerations in developing your company's next generation of leaders. As will be discussed at greater length in chapter 6, each of these three strategies plays a different role:

- Mentoring by senior company executives helps to acculturate the individual, provide career advice, and establish the types of dialogue that develop wisdom in the individual.
- Coaching, whether provided internally or externally, can help the individual focus on specific behavioral and knowledge requirements beyond the scope of the formal LDP.
- Reinforcement of learning helps participants retain and apply what they have learned, not only in terms of specific action-learning projects but also to their everyday work. Reinforcement can come from managers, peers, employees, other LDP participants, or HR and training staff.

Through mentoring, coaching, and reinforcement, as well as through dialogues within and without the classroom with subject matter experts and other instructors, LDP participants will participate in the types of dialogue and discussion that lead to the development of personal wisdom (Stage IV of the learning model).

Together, the four components of the LDP model can provide your company with a comprehensive plan that will ensure that you have the talent you need to sustain and grow your company in the future. While each of the four components can have great value in and of itself, it is the power of the combination of all four that will help you build your company's next generation of leaders.

Summary

This chapter briefly described the four major components of the LDP and used the model of the four stages of learning to show how the LDP is structured to move participants through all four stages, from data to wisdom, and to prepare them for future leadership roles in the company. The important point here is ensuring that all parts of your LDP are directly related to the learning needs of the participants and to the company's business needs.

The next chapters will examine in greater depth each of the four components and how you can plan and implement them in your company. We will start with the LDP education sessions.

Chapter 3

LDP Education Sessions

What's In This Chapter

- How should you select topics?
- How do you identify faculty resources?
- How do you reinforce learning?
- What other educational activities can be used?
- Is there an alternative model for educating the company's high-potentials?

There are hundreds of leadership gurus in the marketplace, all with their own books, their own educational programs, and their own secrets of becoming a great leader. You can learn the leadership secrets of Abraham Lincoln, Attila the Hun, Billy Graham, Colin Powell, Jack Welch, or Santa Claus. You can find books with five or six or seven or 101 steps to becoming a great leader or a list of 21 irrefutable laws of leadership. There is no dearth of advice.

If hiring the best-known, most-expensive leadership guru to train a company's future leaders is an advantage, then large companies that have large leadership development groups and even larger budgets for this purpose have a real edge. But few small to mid-sized companies have the budget for this approach. This chapter discusses education delivery methods, how to select topics for your education sessions, how to identify and recruit faculty (internal and external), and how to structure education sessions to reap optimal learning experiences for the LDP participants and for the company.

Any LDP you create should focus on creating well-rounded leaders who

- know how to lead people
- understand your organization's business and the major business processes that enable work to get done
- think strategically and know how to create and execute the strategic plans needed to ensure your organization's future success
- encourage creative thinking and how to take creative ideas and turn them into innovative products, services, and business methods
- understand marketing and the role of the organization's leaders in effectively marketing the products and services the organization provides to its customers
- are rooted in the organization's culture and are living examples of the organization's values.

If you want to develop your organization's next generation of leaders, enable your employees to gain the required knowledge and skills to become leaders.

Most employees who work their way up the ranks of management or technical leadership are rooted in their specialty areas—they are engineers, accountants, marketers, HR professionals, or call center personnel. As they climb their respective career ladders, their views of the organization's business tend to be myopic—they focus on what is nearest to them—engineers focus on the specifications of products, marketers focus on creating and satisfying customer needs, and call center personnel focus on consumer sales or service. It is through education (and other components of the LDP) that you can help your Hi-Pos gain the knowledge, skills, and perspective that will be needed by future leaders.

Delivering Education to Your High-Potentials

With today's technologies, there are many ways of delivering learning materials to your LDP participants. While they can all be useful for specific purposes, focus the delivery of LDP education sessions on an instructor-led, classroom-based model. There are many reasons for using this strategy:

- It helps participants focus on the content of the educational program. Too often, with self-paced, web-based learning programs, the learning activities are multitasked with other job responsibilities and the learners never really focus on the learning activity.
- It helps learners start building their personal networks throughout the company. You will find that many of the participants already know each other's names from conversations and emails. This is an opportunity for them to really get to know each other and to start working together.
- It helps participants start working together across organizational boundaries. It is best to start this with face-to-face meetings. Later, this collaboration can continue through electronic means, but research has shown great benefits from starting such collaborative efforts with in-person meetings. You will find that the work of the cross-organizational connections made during the LDP education sessions will be useful not only for the action-learning projects that will be assigned following each session, but also in improving cross-functional and cross-geographic collaboration in general.

How technology can be used to complement and supplement the instructor-led, classroom-based education sessions will be discussed later in this chapter, but for now the focus will remain on the content and planning of these face-to-face sessions.

They Get to Check Off the Box

I spoke with a chief learning officer (CLO) at a high-tech firm about leadership development. She spoke of the problem of getting the attention of the company's engineering department. They said that they were too busy to attend any classes, so please would they provide needed training on leading and managing change through a web-based set of modules. The engineers, she was told, knew how to multitask well, and they would all complete the learning assignment. The CLO knew that this was not an optimal solution, but she responded to the department's intransigence by finding a set of eight one-hour web-based modules on the topic.

I asked her what the outcome was. She said that absolutely nothing changed. Most of the engineers paged through the screens as they were working on multiple other tasks, and practically nothing was learned. "They got to check off the box showing that they had completed the training so that it was recorded in our learning management system. Nothing else changed."

Selecting Session Topics

There are so many topics that you can include in your LDP, how are you to choose? Exhibit 3-1 includes a sample of program titles offered by a number of leading business schools in their executive education programs.

Add to the programs listed in exhibit 3-1 the hundreds of leadership programs offered by training vendors and independent consultants and you have a plethora of topics from which to choose, and you could make an argument for the value of every single one of them to your audience of Hi-Pos. Which topics to select depends on a number of variables:

- What are the priorities for topics as determined in your needs analysis (discussions with company executives, surveys of the participants and their managers, and results from 360-degree reviews and other participant assessments)? If, for example, executives' top concern is the participants' lack of understanding of the company's business model, you would want to include a finance-related education session early on.
- How many education sessions do you plan to include in your LDP? Obviously, the more sessions that will be included in the LDP, the more topics you can select. The challenge then is to

Exhibit 3-1. Sample executive education titles from leading business schools.

- Leading for Results
- Leading Successful Change
- The Challenge of Leadership
- Learning to Lead
- High-Performance Leadership
- Leadership as Performance Art
- Human Resources for Strategic Advantage
- Achieving Outstanding Performance
- Customer Focus
- Customer-Focused Innovation
- Managerial Skills for International Business
- Negotiation Dynamics
- Negotiation and Decision-Making Strategies
- Interpersonal Dynamics for High-Performance Executives
- Leading Change and Organizational Renewal
- Managing Teams for Innovation and Success
- The Transition to General Management
- Strategic Business Leadership: Creating and Delivering Value
- Building and Implementing Growth Strategies
- Building, Leading, and Sustaining the Innovative Organization
- Reinventing Your Business Strategy
- Fundamentals of Finance for the Non-Financial Executive
- Understanding and Solving Complex Business Problems
- Strategic Intuition: The Key to Innovation
- Strategic Problem Solving: Developing High-Impact Strategies in Today's Economy

determine a flow for the program—which topics should be presented in which order.

- For any given topic, what action-learning projects can you create to complement each education topic? Every education session should be tied directly to individual or team-based action-learning projects. If you cannot make this connection, you will lose much of the value of the education session.

You need to have a plan for the entire LDP from the start. Questions to be answered in planning the LDP include the following:

- *How long will the LDP last?* It is recommended that your LDP have at least four education sessions over the course of one year. Ideally, the LDP will include eight or nine sessions over a two-year period, with education sessions happening each quarter. Doing programs every three months provides continuity and allows for momentum to build over time. While this could easily be changed to four-month intervals, holding three sessions per year, extending the time between sessions to more than four months usually results in a loss of momentum and enthusiasm among the participants. The one-year time frame allows not only for needed education to be delivered, but also for each participant to be involved with several action-learning projects. The benefits to the company from the networking that will take place among participants will also require several sessions as participants form and work on teams and learn about each other and each other's parts of the business. Further, company executives will be better able to form impressions of the participants if they see them working on a variety of action-learning projects, both individual- and team-based, over a period of a year or two.

- *What topics should be included in the educational sessions?* Create a plan for at least the first three or four sessions from the start. Do not tie yourself to a complete program agenda from the beginning because unforeseen learning needs may arise or the feedback from one session may suggest another topic to be the focus of the next session.

- *How long should each education session last?* As a general rule, plan for each session to last 2.5 to 3.5 days. Some basic schedules for an education session will be presented later in this chapter along with ideas on how to make them work in your company. Of course, the length of each session will depend on the subject matter to be covered—some topics require more time than others.

- *Who will lead the educational sessions?* This is a matter of not only choosing faculty, but also selecting who will moderate/facilitate the overall program so as to provide continuity throughout the entire program.
- *Who else, besides the selected faculty, will participate in each session?* There should be some executive presence at every education session to demonstrate executive support for the program. You may also want to have a number of HR business partners or training staff in attendance, especially if these personnel will be providing coaching and ongoing reinforcement during the action-learning projects and throughout the program.
- *How will you identify and assign action-learning projects after each education session?* This will be discussed in the next chapter.
- *What types of assessment instruments will be used in the program?* While all LDPs optimally include a 360-degree assessment for each participant, there are many other assessment instruments on the market that may be included in various education sessions. Chapter 5 will provide guidance on the selection and use of 360-degree assessments while guidelines for other types of assessments will be provided in chapter 7.
- *How will you reinforce the application of learning to the participants' work and follow up on action-learning assignments?*

Once you have created an outline for the overall LDP, you will need to begin planning the first session. Below are some specific steps you can take to plan the first LDP session and advice on how that initial session should be structured. Additional advice on planning and structuring subsequent LDP education sessions is also given.

Planning Your First Session

As a general rule-of-thumb, focus your first LDP education session on helping participants understand what it means to be leaders and make conscious choices as to whether this is the right career path for them. You can include the following topics in the first session:

- what it means to be a leader, including risks and rewards
- what it takes to become a leader
- some type of self-assessment on leadership skills
- career choices and work–life balance.

At the end of this session, the action-learning project will focus on each participant creating a personal leadership vision statement. This assignment will help them focus on the direction of their careers and their lives and will help the company better understand the aspirations of these Hi-Pos. The personal vision statement should include the following:

- personal aspirations for the participant's career in the company
- personal aspirations for the participant's nonworking life
- areas of development the participant feels are most important for future success
- how the participant anticipates creating a work–life balance.

Selecting Faculty

There are thousands of people who would love to teach in your LDP. There are business school faculty, training vendors, consultants, authors, and speakers who are anxious to be hired by you to teach your Hi-Pos whatever you want them to be taught. You also have the options of using company executives, HR staff, and trainers to conduct the education sessions. How do you choose from so many options?

Your screening of potential faculty (both internal and external) should include research and discussions with candidates related to their

- positions as internal or external faculty
- professional qualifications
- teaching experiences
- responsiveness to your needs
- ability to preview their work
- costs.

Internal vs. External Faculty

In selecting faculty for an educational session, you have many choices:

- external professors, consultants, or training providers
- company executives or subject matter experts
- HR or training staff.

External Faculty

There are hundreds, if not thousands, of external faculty from whom to choose. Often, participants will be more impressed with the program if you select well-known names or professors from a well-known business school to teach them. While these people may not be any better prepared to lead an educational session for you than your available internal resources, just their association with a university or their having written a book on the subject matter gives them instant credibility. This can be very frustrating to any internal subject matter experts you may have in your company, for while they may have as much knowledge and skill in the subject matter and may be as effective teachers as external faculty, they may not possess the credibility factor of a well-known external expert.

Another advantage of using external faculty is that they will undoubtedly have more experience conducting education sessions, because that is their main business. With even the most capable company executives or subject matter experts, their main work is not teaching. You also will generally find that external faculty will be more responsive to your special requests. Because you are paying them, and because conducting educational programs is a major source of income for them, they are more likely to take the time to listen and respond to your specific needs.

Finally, in selecting external faculty, you may want to talk with company executives about their favorite consultants. Many times, the CEO or another company executive may have been working with a particular external consultant for a number of years, and, because of this, the consultant already has a deep understanding of the company and the directions in which the executive is trying to take the company. The executive may welcome an opportunity to have this consultant conduct an LDP education session because it will help align the LDP participants with the executive's vision for the company's future.

Company Executives

Assuming that company executives have the required skills and knowledge with respect to the educational content, there is no better way of impressing your LDP participants with the importance of the content than to have it delivered by a company executive. "If our CFO is going to take three days from her schedule to teach us this, it must be important!"

But for company executives to make effective instructors, they must make the commitment to prepare for the session as an external trainer would and they must clear their schedules to ensure that during the session they are solely focused on teaching. Many programs have been ruined when company executives commit to teaching two-day sessions and announce at the end of the first day that there is an emergency situation, so they won't be there on the second day.

While providing this caveat, it is vital to have company executives deeply involved in your LDP. Rather than having an executive take total responsibility for teaching a session, team the executive with an external faculty member or an internal trainer. In this way, the executive's direct involvement still demonstrates his or her commitment to the program, but the demands on the executive's time are lessened. For example, if you are running a session on how to better engage employees, you might use an external expert teamed with your vice president of HR who can talk about the company's efforts to better engage employees.

Human Resources or Training Staff

In many companies, there are members of the HR or training staff who certainly have the capability to teach an LDP education session. For example, many HR professionals are certified in the Myers-Briggs Type Indicator (MBTI), and a session built around using the MBTI to help participants better understand themselves and others can be a very valuable part of the overall education agenda. Many companies also have trainers on staff who have achieved certification to teach programs from well-known training vendors who offer materials on a variety of relevant topics that can be delivered in one to three days.

The advantages of using internal staff to conduct LDP education sessions include the following:

- faculty who already know the company's business, understand the culture, and can relate to the participants as fellow employees
- lower costs
- readily available internal staff to provide ongoing reinforcement of the subject matter.

Unfortunately in many cases, these internal resources do not carry the credibility of external experts (who may not have any greater expertise). If you want to make effective use of your internal trainers and HR personnel to teach in the LDP, you may need to take a few extra steps to ensure their credibility:

- You can pair the internal trainer with external faculty. The external faculty will lend an air of extra credibility while the internal trainer may gain some added credibility and experience by working with them.
- You can pair the internal trainer with a company executive. The presence of the company executive will add credibility to the use of the internal trainer.
- If you are using a canned program from an external vendor, take the time to customize the module to your company's business and business goals—just as you would ask an external faculty member to do.

Professional Qualifications

Obviously, you only want to hire faculty who have the required professional qualifications with respect to the subject matter of your educational session. Ask them about the following:

- their educational background (not every subject requires someone with a PhD, but faculty should have a substantial amount of education or training on the subject matter)

- their professional experience (you want someone who has real-world experience, rather than someone whose knowledge of the subject matter is limited to surveying what others have done)
- their familiarity with your company and its industry (nothing will turn your audience off more quickly than having faculty who know nothing about your company or its industry and fill the teaching with examples to which your audience cannot relate)
- their familiarity with companies that your company admires or is trying to emulate (try to make certain that the companies you are trying to emulate are in the same league as you; just as your building of the LDP is constrained because you do not have the deep pockets or large leadership development staff of a General Electric or a Honeywell, having the faculty advise participants to do things for which the company has neither the time nor the personnel to do will not be helpful).

Teaching Experience

You want to ensure that the faculty you hire have successful experiences dealing with an audience similar to your group of Hi-Pos:

- Have they taught classes to groups of Hi-Pos before, and what has been their experience with such groups?
- Have they taught in your industry before?
- What teaching methods will they use in the program?
- Do they have teaching materials that you can review?

Responsiveness

Too often you will hear from faculty candidates: "Here's what I do. Let me know if you want to hire me." You want your faculty to be responsive to your specific needs:

- Are they willing to tailor their material to your audience? For example, would they be willing to create a case study based on the work of your company? Or, in a financial analysis class, would they be willing to have the class analyze the financial statements of your company and one or more of its competitors, rather than using whatever financial statements the faculty usually includes? You will also want to check references of other clients of the faculty to ensure that promised customizations are actually done.

- Will the faculty be willing to reinforce the learning from the class in any or all of the following ways:
  — holding a virtual follow-up session two weeks after the education session
  — conducting an executive briefing on the subject matter in conjunction with the LDP education session, live or via videoconference
  — conducting a short briefing/training for the managers of the LDP participants, probably by videoconference?
- Are they willing to interview several LDP participants before the program to ensure that the educational content will match the group's learning needs?
- Are they willing to discuss with the LDP manager the types of action-learning projects that would make good follow-ons to the education session?

Preview

Can you preview the faculty's work? This can be done by getting a video of a class the faculty has presented to another client or, even better, by viewing the faculty in front of a live audience (another client or a business school executive education program) in person. You have had the experience of meeting a college professor who is brilliant, charming in person, has written highly acclaimed books, and is a successful consultant, but who cannot teach well. The last thing you want to do is to hire someone to give one of your education sessions who will bore your audience. And the only way to ensure that your teaching candidate will do a great job with your audience is to preview that person doing a similar session for another audience.

Costs

All companies are concerned with how great an investment they will have to make in their leadership development efforts. Most small to mid-sized companies do not have the deep pockets of the well-known large companies that are lauded for their LDPs. So, how much is this going to cost? More cost considerations are discussed in chapter 10. Below are some costs to consider:

- What are the faculty's fees and estimates of related expenses?
- Are there additional fees for participant materials or assessment instruments the faculty may want to use in the session?
- Does the instruction require special equipment, such as computer and network arrangements for a simulation exercise?
- Will the faculty need any additional support to conduct the class, such as a technician for computer equipment or a second instructor/facilitator/observer for parts of the session?

Structuring the Session

You are asking your participants to take several days away from their work (which they will have to do when they get back to their offices) to attend each LDP education session. You want to make certain they feel that every session they attend is worth their investment of time. So, how do you structure your sessions to best use that time? This is especially important for the first LDP education session, because first impressions count for a lot.

The First LDP Session

A suggested structure for the first LDP education session is shown in figure 3-1.

Start the first education session with a sit-down dinner on Sunday evening. (The days of the week you choose for your program should fit with your company's culture.) This is an informal way of letting the participants get to know each other, and a good dinner always makes people feel welcome. It is recommended that you use place cards for the seating so that each table has a mix of participants from different business units, functional areas, and geographies—this will help them start building their personal networks within the company.

Figure 3-1. First education session.

	Sunday	Monday	Tuesday	Wednesday
Morning		Education session #1	Education session #3	Team planning session
Afternoon		Education session #2	Education session #4 + assignment of action-learning projects	Adjourn
Evening	Welcome dinner	Dinner with assigned teams	Dinner with company executives	

After dinner, the LDP manager (who will provide continuity throughout the entire LDP) should welcome the participants, have the participants introduce themselves to each other (using one of many possible ice-breaker techniques), handle logistics announcements, and then introduce the company's CEO.

The CEO should welcome the participants and emphasize that the company is making a major investment in their future by creating the LDP. Following the CEO, the vice president of HR (or another executive if that executive is sponsoring the program) should also welcome the audience and, at the same time, give the participants a dose of reality:

- The participants have been designated as having high potential for future leadership positions in the company, but being included in the program is not a guarantee of success or of future promotions. Future success will depend on each participant's performance in the program while still accomplishing his or her day jobs as well as on the availability of open positions at any point in time. Some may complete the program and never get promoted; some may be dropped from the program for nonperformance; some may choose to leave the company voluntarily.

- While the company is investing in their future, participants are expected to invest in their future with the company. The company is asking for a commitment that the participants complete the entire (one-year or two-year) program and stay with the company for at least two years after the program is completed. (Check with your legal department as to whether this expectation is enforceable under country or local labor laws, but often just setting the expectation is sufficient to make the point that the company is looking for an equal commitment from the participants in whom they are investing so much time, effort, and resources.)

Following breakfast Monday morning, the moderator will call the education session to order. Use place cards to assemble the participants into their action-learning teams (predetermined to allow for maximum interaction among business units, functions, and geographies). Participants will stay with their teams throughout this education session, working together on group exercises and action-learning assignments as scheduled. (This will help participants build their personal and working relationships with each other.) The moderator will handle any logistics announcements and then introduce the faculty who will conduct the session.

Rather than have a formal dinner Monday evening, plan for the assigned teams to have dinner together to start getting to know each other.

On Tuesday, the faculty will continue the educational program, finishing the formal presentations sometime on Tuesday afternoon. At the conclusion of the formal education program, the faculty and the program moderator can jointly instruct the participant teams on their action-learning assignments, explaining the guidelines for the projects, the timelines, the required products, and how the projects are to be presented at the start of the next education session. If coaches are going to be assigned to each team, those assignments can be announced along with an explanation of the role of the coaches, who will periodically check on team progress and be available to answer questions and help overcome any obstacles that the team may encounter in working on the action-learning projects.

On Tuesday evening, plan a more informal dinner for the participants. A number of company executives can be invited to join in for informal conversation with the participants. This provides an opportunity for these executives to get to know these Hi-Pos who have probably not been in their line of vision in their regular jobs.

On Wednesday morning, there is no formal education session. Rather, teams are expected to meet to plan their action-learning projects, determining logistics such as how the members will work together and how they will keep each other informed of progress. If the action-learning teams have been assigned coaches, the coaches may participate in these team meetings. The one expectation that should be set for the Wednesday morning session is that, within a week, each team will complete and submit the action-planning project description form that will be discussed in chapter 4.

Subsequent LDP Sessions

Each subsequent education session should build on the last. As explained earlier, there is a wide array of possible topics from which to choose. The appendix contains brief descriptions of a dozen possible topics, along with ideas for the types of action-learning projects that could accompany each. The list of business school executive education program titles in exhibit 3-1 can also provide many ideas. Again, focus each selected topic on specific needs of the audience and of the company. The recommended structure for each subsequent LDP education session generally follows the same pattern as the first session (see figure 3-2) with two additions:

- reporting on the previous action-learning projects on Sunday afternoon
- dinner and an open question-and-answer session with a company executive on Tuesday evening.

Action-Learning Projects Reports

On Sunday afternoon, the participants will report on the action-learning projects they undertook at the completion of the last session. The reporting

Figure 3-2. Subsequent education sessions.

	Sunday	Monday	Tuesday	Wednesday
Morning		Education session #1	Education session #3	Education session #5 + assignment of action-learning projects
Afternoon	Reports on action-learning projects	Education session #2	Education session #4	Team planning meetings and adjourn
Evening	Welcome dinner	Dinner with assigned teams	Dinner with company executive	

will take the form of short (6- to 10-minute) presentations to a panel of company executives, with a few more minutes allowed for the panel to ask questions. If the action-learning projects were individual projects, rather than team projects, it may be necessary to have the reporting happen in two or more rooms to allow enough time for each presentation. Guidelines for these presentations are discussed in chapter 4.

Dinner and Q&A with Company Executive

For each LDP education session, starting with the second session, invite a company executive to have dinner with the participants on Tuesday evening. Following the dinner, the executive can speak for a short time (15 to 20 minutes) about his or her own leadership journey, about the company's and his or her own history, and about the opportunities awaiting the company and the participants in the future.

Following this presentation, the executive can open the floor to questions—about anything and everything that the audience wants to discuss—and this discussion should continue until it is finished. These types of sessions are invaluable both to the participants and to the executive. For the participants, it is a chance to get to know one of the company executives whom they have rarely if ever met and to learn more about the company's history, culture, and vision for the future. For the executive, it is an opportunity to learn about what is concerning this group of highly regarded employees from throughout the company (and not just in the executive's domain) and to learn about what it is like on the front lines.

The CEO's Late Night

The company's founder and CEO retired from the CEO slot just as the LDP began. The former COO, a much younger man, had been named the new CEO. Because he was spending so much time getting established in his new role, he could not find the time to attend the first two sessions. Finally, he agreed to attend the third session, this one being held on a college campus.

He had been briefed on the audience and what he was to cover—to talk about his own leadership journey, his own and the company's history, and his vision for the future of the company. Then, he was to take questions for as long as the questions lasted.

Dinner finished around 8:30 p.m. The CEO concluded his remarks around 9:00 p.m., and then he started taking questions. At 10:30 p.m., the catering manager came in and said that his crew needed to clean the room and that the meeting would have to move. The CEO asked where he could move it, and the catering manager agreed to have someone open the college pub next door. The meeting moved next door. The questions and discussions continued. At 1:00 a.m., the pub manager said that he had to close down and go home. The CEO bought the rest of the keg, and the discussions continued until 4:30 a.m., with no one leaving.

The next day, the CEO and the participants unanimously said it was one of the best experiences they had ever had. From that point on, the CEO did not miss another session of the LDP.

The session model in figure 3-2 concludes on Wednesday afternoon. Of course, the actual schedule will vary depending on the content of the program and how much planning time is needed for the next round of action-learning projects.

External Programs

As will be discussed in chapter 10, the cost of running an internal LDP can be much less than sending your Hi-Pos to a series of external programs at business schools and other training vendors. At certain times, it may be necessary to send individual participants to external training to meet individual learning needs as specified in their IDPs.

In the LDP model, there is a place for external training for all participants. If you have designed an LDP with nine quarterly sessions over a two-year period, ideally, for the eighth session, you would send each participant to an external program, rather than holding a group gathering. The reasons for this are as follows:

- Because every LDP participant is unique, and each has an IDP, each will have some learning need that will not be included in the formal LDP agenda. Putting in a placeholder for an external learning program can help fill these individual learning needs.
- While you have designed the LDP to build a cohesive group of next-generation leaders, there is a potential danger from having the participants interact only with each other and limiting their view of the outside world. By sending participants to a variety of public learning programs, they will be exposed to ideas, points of view, and approaches from other companies, and this can only help them.
- The action-learning assignment to be completed after this external session should be for the participants to update their personal vision statements (originally developed after the first education session). Their presentation at the final LDP session should be on this vision statement as well as on what they have learned from their experience in the LDP.

Another common model for LDPs is to contract with a business school for a week of training, usually annually, for a group of Hi-Pos from your company. The program is typically residential at the business school or at a university conference center and includes multiple business school faculty presenting on a variety of subjects during the week. There are also team assignments during the week, whether they are business school case studies or company-specific planning projects, with the week culminating in a series of team presentations to the faculty and company executives. Figure 3-3 shows an outline of a typical weeklong program.

Advantages

There are two primary advantages of using the business-school model. First and foremost is the coordination among the various faculty that you should expect (but don't always get) from the business school with which you have contracted. Almost all business schools have an executive education arm that designs, sells, and coordinates these types of programs. They will typically have a lot of experience putting together these types of special programs and can provide invaluable assistance with program design.

Second, using this once-a-year, weeklong business-school model will greatly reduce the company's planning, logistics, and administrative burden. Instead of planning three or four events a year, you now have only one per year to accomplish, and you have the staff of the business school and the university's conference center to handle a lot of the administrative details, from providing materials to arranging equipment and room setup to choosing menus.

Disadvantages

There are a number of disadvantages of using the annual, weeklong, business-school model compared with the LDP model presented in this book:

- The program may be too intense to allow for real learning. Because you are jamming so many topics into such a short period of time, you run the risk of overwhelming the audience, thereby reducing retention of the material.
- The business-school model has no reinforcement of learning built in. Once the program is over, it's over—there is no ongoing reinforcement of learning through action-learning projects and the other methods of reinforcement built into the LDP model.

53

Figure 3-3. Model of a weeklong business school LDP.

	Sunday	Monday	Tuesday	Wednesday	Thursday	Friday
Morning		Leadership session #1	Finance session #1	Strategic planning	SWOT analysis	Team presentations
Afternoon		Leadership session #2	Finance session #2	Creative thinking skills	Team project working group	Adjourn
Evening	Opening dinner	Evening work assignment	Team case analysis	Team project working group	Team project working group	

SWOT = strengths, weaknesses, opportunities, and threats.

- The business-school model does not allow for ongoing teamwork among the participants. While the participants will all meet each other, and will work together on the assigned team project during the week, the LDP model enables participants to continue working together over time, to build their networks and relationships on an ongoing basis.

- Executive involvement in the business-school model is generally limited to hearing the final presentations on Friday, with the executives flying in and out quickly to accomplish this. With the LDP model, executives get to see the participants in action, working on a variety of projects over an extended period of time.

- When you select a business school with which to partner, you are generally going to be limited to the topics and approaches of that school's faculty (although business schools sometimes show more flexibility about including topics and speakers from outside their own realm if the customer insists). With the LDP model, you are able to select topics and faculty to match your company's specific needs.

- When you contract with a business school, your costs are almost certain to increase because you are paying for the overhead of the business school and the university's conference center. Typically, the cost of the faculty in the program will be two or three times what it would cost your company to hire the same faculty as independent consultants. (More on cost considerations will be found in chapter 10.)

The Sessions Just Get Better and Better!

When I designed and ran my first LDP, I was gratified when many of the participants told me how great the first session was. I was equally pleased when they responded well to the second session. But an interesting pattern emerged—after each session, participants told me that the latest session was "the best yet!"

All of the sessions were good—very good in fact. I had done a lot of research and had selected relevant topics and great faculty. But did they really get better each quarter? What was happening here was not that the sessions were getting better, but that the participants were getting more from each subsequent session due to the following:

- their trust in the program (at the first few meetings, participants were uncertain how much value they would get from the programs, but after several sessions, they knew that the program was designed to help them and their careers)
- their comfort working with each other (as the participants worked with each other in class and on action-learning projects, they learned to trust each other more and started forming personal relationships with each other that enabled them to learn and work more effectively together)
- their seeing how all of the parts fit together (the design of the program had each session build on previous sessions, so that the participants could see the added value of each new topic).

So, the education sessions did not keep getting better and better, but the participants got more value from each one as the program progressed. This won't happen with the once-a-year, one-week, business-school model.

Reinforcing Learning

Very often, after learning something new in a classroom setting, the program participants think they get it, but later discover one or more of the following:

- They misunderstood what was taught.
- Because they had never tried the new method or tried to apply some new information, they didn't know what questions to ask.
- As they tried to implement what they learned, they ran into an unforeseen obstacle and got stuck.

In each of these circumstances, participants often abandon the new (and hopefully better) way of doing things and revert to old methods and knowledge that are familiar and reliable—they may not be as good, but they know them and know how to make them work.

To overcome this frequent circumstance, two weeks after each education session hold a virtual follow-up session.

Virtual Follow-Up Sessions

Virtual follow-up sessions are conducted via teleconference or videoconference with the faculty from the recently completed education session. The purpose of the session is to help participants apply what they have learned to transform the information they received into their personal knowledge (moving from Stage II to Stage III in the four stages of learning). In this session, the faculty can answer such questions as the following:

- "I thought I understood what you meant by X, but now I'm not so sure. Can you go over that again?"
- "Now that I'm trying to apply this in the real world, I find that I forgot to ask about Y. How does Y figure into this?"
- "Things were going great with my implementation until Z happened. How do I get through or around Z?"

The session can be facilitated by polling the LDP participants a few days before the actual live session so that the faculty can understand and prepare to answer the issues that are most important to the participants. Most companies already have the technology in place to hold teleconferences and videoconferences, so setting up the follow-up session can be easily accomplished. The participation of the faculty in the session is vital and should be negotiated as part of the faculty contract for the education session. Given that there is no travel involved, there should be no additional fee from the faculty for holding the session. A virtual follow-up session will typically run from 60 to 90 minutes.

Reinforcement of Learning on the Job

The action-learning projects (described in chapter 4) that will be assigned at the end of each education session are the primary means of reinforcing the learning that will take place in each session. At the same time, it can also be very helpful to reinforce the learning through other means.

While the LDP participants are doing their LDP-related projects, they still have day jobs to accomplish, and many may find that what they have learned through the LDP can and should be transferred to their day-to-day work. Very often, at the conclusion of an LDP education session, participants will comment that "my manager could really use this" or "all of the company's executives should learn this." Without the support of the participants' managers and company executives, change is less likely to extend beyond the specific projects on which the participants work. There are several ways to overcome this challenge:

- You can have the program faculty conduct a separate education session for company executives or, at a minimum, provide a briefing to those executives. Not only will this help reinforce the learning for the LDP participants, but it also demonstrates the executives' commitment to the goals of the LDP.

- You can have the program faculty brief the managers of LDP participants on what they are learning and how they are expected to use it on their jobs. Additionally, you can offer to provide training on the new methods/skills/knowledge to those managers. By doing this, you are removing an often-perceived threat that the LDP participants are going to bypass or over-rule their managers.

- You can identify subject matter experts in the company who can act as coaches on new methods/skills/knowledge for the LDP participants. The subject matter experts can be from the HR group, the training group, or anywhere in the company where the needed expertise resides. This can be done formally or informally, face-to-face, via phone or email, or in a discussion forum on the company's intranet.

- You can engage the program faculty to participate in a periodic series of telephone or electronic conferences with participants to reinforce their learning and provide ongoing coaching, or you can ask the faculty to periodically check on questions posted on an LDP discussion board.

- You can set up a discussion board for LDP participants to support and reinforce their learning with each other.

Each education component of the LDP has three parts:

1. the formal education session
2. the virtual follow-up session
3. the reinforcement of learning on the job.

This combination, as shown in figure 3-4, is designed to optimize learning and to facilitate the movement across the four levels of learning.

Supplementing LDP Education Activities

The development of your Hi-Pos does not have to be limited to the program model presented in this chapter. There are several ways to supplement the LDP with related learning activities. First, because each LDP participant will have an IDP, there may be a need to send one or more participants to other trainings that are not part of the overall LDP curriculum. For example, you may have a brilliant finance manager who has absolutely atrocious presentation skills or you may have an outstanding marketing manager whose native language is not English and is very difficult to understand. In these cases, these individuals can be sent to programs to help develop the skills they need.

Here are some ways you can supplement the LDP agenda to help build skills and, just as important, build the LDP community:

Figure 3-4. Reinforcement.

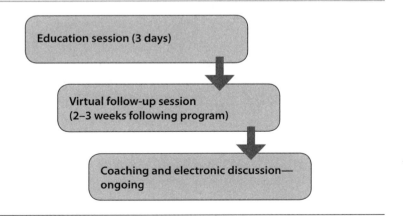

- **Webcasts.** There are many cost-free webcasts with excellent content available in the web market. If LDP managers see an upcoming webcast that fits well with the current LDP agenda, they can advertise it to the LDP participants. Better, by establishing an LDP discussion forum, you can set up a discussion of the webcast among the participants, perhaps starting with a general question or two, to stimulate their thinking and discussion—even better would be to get a company executive to sponsor and participate in the discussion of the webcast with the participants.

- **Books.** You can distribute a book or an article on a topic of interest to all LDP participants, using the discussion forum (with or without executive sponsorship) to spark discussions. You can also expand this type of book club beyond the LDP audience. If you find a book that you think will be of interest or value to your company's CEO or other officers, send a copy of the book to them with a note explaining why you think it would be of interest. Sometimes this effort gets ignored, but other times the CEO may ask you to get copies sent to the staff and then to lead a discussion of the topic at an executive committee meeting.

- **Discussion Forum.** Set up a general discussion forum for the LDP participants where they can ask each other questions, bounce ideas off each other, and generally coach each other to reinforce their learning in a safe environment.

- **Parent Companies.** When a company is bought by another company, there may be many changes made or the new parent may leave its acquisition alone to run its own show. If you find your company has been acquired by a larger company, don't forget to look at your new parent's resources for developing leaders. It may be that your parent company already has an LDP in place and you only need to ask to get some of your Hi-Pos included in that program. Or it may be that the parent company already has a number of in-house leadership and management development courses that you could bring in as part of your own LDP. You'll never know unless you ask.

Keep in mind, if you are conducting the LDP on a quarterly basis with challenging action-learning projects in between sessions, adding too many of these other activities can start to overwhelm your participants.

Summary

The LDP education session model presented in this chapter is the cornerstone of an effective LDP to help your company develop its next generation of leaders. This chapter discussed how to structure LDP education sessions and how to reinforce learning from each session through the use of virtual follow-up sessions and other methods. Equally important is the assignment of action-learning projects following each education session, and these projects are the subject of the next chapter.

Chapter 4

LDP Experiential and Action Learning

What's In This Chapter

- What defines experiential and action learning?
- How do you use action-learning projects to reinforce learning from the LDP education sessions?
- How do LDP participants report on their action-learning projects?

Experiential and action learning help leadership development program participants move from the information stage to the knowledge and wisdom stages. By applying what they have learned through the education sessions to action-learning projects, they take the information from those sessions and turn it into personal knowledge. And by applying that knowledge to their regular work and to experiential-learning assignments, LDP participants have the opportunity to reflect on how the lessons they have learned relate to different types of situations, which helps them develop their personal wisdom.

This chapter discusses various types of experiential and action learning and how they help develop these high-potentials into your company's next generation of leaders. You will read a number of examples of learning projects and be given guidance on how to select and assign projects to your LDP participants.

Experiential Learning Versus Action Learning

What's the difference between experiential learning and action learning, and how can each fit into your leadership development strategy?

- *Experiential learning* encompasses any change in job assignment that helps an individual develop the knowledge and skills needed for future leadership roles in the company.
- *Action learning* deals with specific individual or team projects that are designed to help LDP participants apply their learning, thereby helping transform the information received in an educational session into personal knowledge.

Experiential Learning

Experiential learning focuses on one individual at a time and involves a new or expanded job role designed to help the individual grow by applying learning to new situations and by testing various personal competencies. Some examples of experiential-learning assignments include the following:

- participating in a cross-functional task force to help broaden the business perspective of the individual
- filling in temporarily for someone who is on leave or for someone who has left
- broadening the perspective on the company's business beyond its home country with an international assignment
- moving temporarily to another group so that the individual better understands the overall business processes (for example, the comptrollers of the engineering and manufacturing divisions

trade jobs for six months so that they can learn about other parts of the business)

- heading up a task team to develop team leadership abilities
- assigning the LDP participant to be a coach or mentor to a new employee.

An experiential-learning assignment can range in scope from filling in for one's manager while the manager takes a few days of vacation to serving on an ad hoc task force to solve a business problem to taking an overseas assignment. The length of such an assignment can range from a few days to several years. Experiential-learning assignments should generally be part of an IDP, as will be discussed in chapter 5. At the same time, there are ways of including some experiential learning in your LDP:

- Schedule one LDP education session to take place in a city where the company is participating in an industry conference or trade show. Assign participants to staff the company's booth, and give them a set of questions to ask current and potential customers who stop by the booth. Alternatively, you can assign each LDP participant to visit a competitor's trade show booth and report on what they saw and heard there. This type of experience can give participants, especially those who work in staff functions, a better understanding of the marketplace and your company's position in that market.
- Assign each LDP participant to participate in a sales call with a prospective customer. While this obviously will require the cooperation of the company's sales organization, it can help the LDP participants broaden their perspective of the company's business and customers.
- Assign teams to participate in college recruiting for the company. This will require the Hi-Pos to learn more about the company and the full range of company activities and opportunities so that they can better represent those opportunities to candidates from those colleges.

Working in Asia

One company planned an LDP education session to take place in Beijing, the company's Asian headquarters. The education session dealt with doing business internationally. The education session itself started on Sunday afternoon and concluded on Tuesday afternoon. The experiential-learning assignment for this session was to have each participant work with the Asian management team to find a productive way of using the rest of the week to better understand and improve the company's Asian business. Some participants consulted with Asian clients. Some trained Asian staff. Others worked with their counterparts in the Asian organization to better understand and coordinate the international business.

It was a great experience for the LDP participants. The Asian management team, which often complained of not getting enough attention from company headquarters in the United States, was thrilled to have all of these resources available to them, albeit for only a few days. More important, the LDP participants expanded their personal networks to their Asian counterparts, and this would have been almost impossible for many participants in their normal, day-to-day jobs.

Action Learning

Ideally, action-learning projects are a follow-on to the educational component described in chapter 3. By following an educational program with an action-learning project, you do the following:

- Give participants in your LDP the opportunity to test what they have learned, thereby reinforcing the learning that took place.
- See how well LDP participants can follow through on their learning and apply what they have learned to these projects.
- Create new synergies with Hi-Pos working below the executive level of the company.
- Build the business knowledge and acumen of participants.
- Solve some long-standing challenges that will help the company improve operations today and in the future.
- Test the leadership skills of the LDP participants.

Benefits of Experiential and Action Learning

There are many ways experiential and action learning can yield benefits to the LDP participants and to the company as a whole.

Using Learning on the Job

Too often, when training participants are asked about the results of their learning efforts, they respond: "I learned a lot that could have potential benefits to me, my group, and the company. But I got back to the office and while I had changed, nothing else had changed. The job was the same, my workload was even larger because work had accumulated while I was away, my boss wanted me to get my regular job done before even thinking about changing anything. I never had the opportunity to apply what I had learned. Business as usual!"

It is a basic tenet of adult learning theory that adult learners want and need the opportunity to use what they have learned, and that is the goal of action-learning projects. The faster they have the opportunity to apply what they have learned, the greater the retention of that learning. Unfortunately, expenditures on training often seem like "The Great Training Robbery" to both the participants and the company management— when training is not applied to the job to make a positive difference in individual, team, and company business result, the investment in that training is wasted.

Testing Follow-Through

There is a basic expectation that the employees designated as Hi-Pos will follow through on their learning, applying that learning to make a positive difference in their own, their groups', and their company's business performance. The assignment of action-learning projects following educational sessions gives you the opportunity to test participants' follow-through skills. Will they make the extra effort expected from the company's future leaders? Will they develop effective plans to execute their projects? Will they find ways of overcoming or obviating the obstacles to their projects that will inevitably arise during execution?

The answer is that some of the participants will succeed and some won't. When participants report back on their projects at the end of the allotted time, you should expect that while most will be successful, some will not have succeeded. Does this mean that those who have not succeeded should be dropped from the program? Not necessarily. If participants were not successful, ask them to explain the reasons for their failure (or suboptimal results) and ask both what they learned from the experience and what they would do differently if they knew at the beginning of the project what they know today. (Later, this chapter will discuss how to structure participants' reporting on projects.) Failure on an action-learning project should not be sufficient grounds for dismissal from the program or for dropping the person from the high-potential group; however, failure to learn from an unsuccessful project is a sufficient reason for either or both actions.

Creating New Synergies

After the first session of one LDP, several participants commented that even if there had been no educational program, the synergies created by bringing together the participants, just having them meet each other and having the opportunity to learn about each other's business challenges and how they were meeting those challenges, would have been worth the company's investment.

Too often, communication between different business units and functional groups is focused on the top executives who may or may not meet regularly. This slows down the business because it takes time for an individual within a business unit to send a question up the ladder, have the head of the unit communicate with a peer, and then have the peer send the message down to the right person within the other business unit, and then to reverse the process to answer the question. Through the LDP, your company can help knock down those impediments to cross-functional or cross-business-unit communications, thus creating synergies at lower levels of the organization. Additionally, when LDP participants are eventually promoted to leadership positions within the company, they will already have started building their cross-functional, cross-business unit networks.

======================

Solving Problems at a Lower Level

One of the company's business units was having a banner sales year in North America, but very poor sales in the European region. The head of the business unit and the head of sales in Europe had never had a good relationship, and it was reflected in the poor European sales numbers for this particular product line.

At one session of the company's LDP, the business unit's engineering manager had dinner with one of the European sales managers and asked why her group wasn't selling the group's products. The answer was that the salespeople were anxious to sell the products but had a number of questions about them and needed some training on the product line. She had requested this training through the head of sales but never got any response. Within weeks, the engineering manager arranged to fly to Europe with the group's marketing manager to train the European sales force. This was done by these mid-level managers without the involvement of either the business unit manager or the European sales manager. In the next year, European sales of this product line exceeded those in North America.

======================

Building Business Acumen

Most of the Hi-Pos in your LDP will have grown up within their functional areas—they will be engineering managers, marketing managers, finance managers, sales managers, and so on. They will be in the LDP because of the excellence of their work *within their functional areas of expertise.* As their responsibilities broaden, they need to expand their worldviews. As a wise man once said, if your only tool is a hammer, the whole world looks like a nail. For example, an engineer gets satisfaction from producing state-of-the-art products that include all of the latest bells and whistles. But if this measure of engineering excellence produces products that customers aren't ready to buy or cost too much to manufacture, the company's sales will suffer, even though the engineer, from the point of view of engineering excellence, is doing a great job. Similarly, an attorney may spend months negotiating with a potential business partner, insisting that every word and punctuation mark in a partnership agreement

Giving Participants Time to Talk

Because bringing participants together is so costly to the company, and because it happens so infrequently, there is a natural tendency to cram as much information as possible into the available time. So, early in my career, when planning a company-wide training where we were bringing people in from all over the world, I would schedule every available minute: We had speakers at breakfast, lunch, and dinner, and late-evening presentations, working the participants 12 or more hours a day. It seemed like the best way to maximize the company's investment in training.

But it wasn't.

What I learned quickly was that working participants 12 or more hours a day burns them out and reduces retention of the material. I also discovered from the participants that *more than half of the learning that takes place at any learning event comes from the informal, unstructured interaction of participants with each other.* It doesn't matter how excellent the planned training is, more learning takes place informally than from formal instruction.

So, while you want the formal training to be worthwhile, you need to plan time for the informal interactions to take place. Below are some guidelines for scheduling this valuable down time:

- Don't schedule speakers or other activities at more than one meal a day. Often, I will plan for the CEO or another top executive to speak with participants after dinner one evening (to best fit the executive's schedule), but I will leave other mealtimes without any formal agenda, other than program announcements.
- In a multiday program, give participants an opportunity to leave the training premises for dinner at least one evening. If I am going to assign team-based action-learning projects, I tell participants early who will be on each team and suggest that each team have dinner together one evening to get to know each other better.
- When assigning team-based action-learning projects, I schedule time toward the end of the session for the teams to start their planning. While I encourage the teams to use tele- or video-conferences, discussion forums, wikis, and other groupware to accomplish their work, giving the teams time to plan together in a person-to-person format at the start of a project pays great dividends to team productivity.

be perfect. This is what attorneys are trained to do. At the same time, the company's sales or market position may suffer greatly because of the delay caused by endless negotiations over inconsequential wording.

Action-learning projects enable participants to work with people from different business units, functional areas, and geographies and to learn from them about their work methods, their areas of expertise, and the challenges they are facing. Aside from the projects themselves, just building the relationships with people in other functional areas and geographies can help all participants better understand the scope of the company's business and the challenges being faced throughout the company.

Solving Long-standing Challenges

Every organization has long-standing challenges that remain unsolved because the organization never gives those problems a high enough priority to assign people to solve them. In large, prosperous companies, these types of challenges are often met by throwing large numbers of people and large amounts of money at the problems until they are solved. But small to mid-sized companies often go for years facing challenges that have never become vital enough to the company's business to use scarce resources to solve.

The Same Old Problems

One of my first jobs in the corporate world was as a curriculum manager for software services technicians at Digital Equipment Corporation. The group to which I belonged held quarterly management meetings, bringing in about a dozen managers from around the world for several days to make plans, discuss challenges, and make decisions.

After I had been in the group for a year, the group was moving offices to another area in the training complex. Our manager, in cleaning up his office to prepare for the move, found the minutes from the quarterly meetings from six and seven years earlier. In examining these minutes, we discovered that the same issues that were stumping us at the present time were also being discussed years ago. For example, there was an ongoing problem with finding enough qualified instructors. The problem was not insoluble. It was just that it was never a high enough priority, compared to other issues, to get the group to act on the problem, so we continued to muddle through.

U.S. President Dwight Eisenhower once said that only two types of memos reached his desk: those marked "urgent" and those marked "important." He complained that so much time was spent on the urgent issues that there was never time to pay attention to what was important.

In every organization, there are similar issues—ones that are important but never urgent enough to get the attention they need to get them resolved. Check the minutes of your own group's meetings, whether you are on the company's executive committee or in a small work group, and you will find these types of important, but not urgent, issues. These make very good candidates for the LDP's action-learning assignments. A team of Hi-Pos, or an individual participant, can often find solutions to such problems (if given the right tools and empowerment), thereby benefitting the organization. And if they cannot solve the problem, the organization is no worse off than before.

=====================

These types of challenges make ideal action-learning projects for the LDP's individual participants and teams. They often perfectly complement an educational session on creative thinking, critical thinking, or business process reengineering, allowing the participants to put what they have learned to work for the benefit of the organization.

You can ask executives and managers throughout the organization to nominate projects, or you can ask the participants to come up with their own project ideas. Of course, you have to set boundaries for these projects so that they do not exceed the time and manpower available, as will be discussed in a later section of this chapter.

Testing Leadership and Teamwork Skills

Action-learning projects also give you the opportunity to observe how well participants work as part of a team and to see who steps up to lead each team. This is another test of participants' readiness for promotion, and the beauty is that you get to test them *before* you make an unfortunate promotional error.

There are several ways of observing these behaviors, including having an HR manager (or other manager) act as a coach and observer for each assigned team or having team members rate each other at the end of each team project. These methods will be discussed at greater length in chapter 7.

Some further examples of experiential- and action-learning projects, for teams and individuals, are found in exhibits 4-1 and 4-2.

Will the Real Leader Please Stand Up?

At the start of one education session, teams of participants reported to a group of senior executives on their just-completed action-learning projects assigned at the previous session. All of the teams had put together excellent projects with impressive results.

At the conclusion of one team's presentation, the team leader challenged the senior executives: "Now that we have put in all of this great work, what are *you* going to do to ensure that what we have started here gets wider circulation in the company? We have demonstrated that our approach can yield great results for the business. What are *you* going to do to continue our great work?"

The next team to present had an equally worthwhile project with similarly good results. At the conclusion of the team's presentation, the team leader told the executives: "We believe that what we have started here can yield even greater benefits if the process we created is replicated in other parts of the company. Because of this, we have documented the process and shared the document with our peers throughout the company. We have also told them that all members of the team are available to answer questions and coach them through the process. We already have four other groups interested in adopting the process we created."

To which team will the executives look to fill leadership slots?

Exhibit 4-1. Team experiential/action-learning projects.

- Analyze a competitor.
- Design a new product or service.
- Develop a new marketing campaign.
- Lead a General Electric–style workout session.
- Lead an after-action review.
- Start an employee newsletter.
- Start a customer newsletter.
- Determine how to better engage employees.
- Conduct a customer survey.
- Start a book club.
- Prepare a change introduction plan.
- Plan a trade show exhibit.
- Lead the company's United Way campaign.

Action-Learning Projects

How do you define and assign action-learning projects to LDP participants? Several factors need to be considered:

- defining project scope
- tying projects to educational topics
- assigning or selecting projects.

Defining Project Scope

Because the LDP and any assignments arising from the LDP are in addition to the participants' regular workload, you need to limit the scope of each action-learning project to what can reasonably be expected to be accomplished, first, within the time span before the next scheduled educational session (typically three months), and, second, with the extra workload you can expect the participants to assume in addition to their regular jobs (typically 10 to 15 percent or four to six hours per week).

The scope will also depend on whether you are assigning individual projects or team projects—in the latter case, you can multiply the number of hours available by the number of people on the team.

Exhibit 4-2. Individual experiential/action-learning projects.

- Teach a class.
- Participate in (or lead) a team:
  - to tackle a cross-functional issue
  - to introduce a new product or service
  - to perform market research.
- Orient and coach a new employee.
- Visit
  - a customer
  - a distributor
  - a remote sales/service office
  - headquarters.
- Analyze a competitor's product or service.
- Go to a trade show:
  - Work at your company's booth.
  - Visit competitors' booths.
  - Make a presentation.
  - Volunteer to help organize the show.
- Attend an industry conference:
  - Make a presentation.
  - Attend competitors' presentations.
  - Talk with customers.
  - Talk with competitors' customers.
- Present a proposal to higher management.
- Plan and supervise an office move.
- Follow a new product or service through its entire life cycle.
- Plan and manage a visit by a customer.
- Plan and manage a visit by a new manager from another site or country.
- Review and evaluate a training.
- Supervise cost-cutting.
- Analyze a business process.
- Work with the IT department to plan a new system.
- Spend a day with an expert (job shadowing).

Note: Some companies choose to reassign LDP participants to a project team, removing them from the responsibilities of their regular jobs for the duration of the project. For example, at one information technology (IT) consulting company, Hi-Pos completed an eight-week, full-time training and then, as a group, were assigned to a pro-bono consulting assignment for an additional eight weeks to take what they learned about the company's consulting model and methodology from the classroom and put it into action. But few small to mid-sized companies have large enough staffs and the depth of resources to support this approach.

Also, because you are testing the learning and capabilities of the LDP participants, and because there is no guarantee that the action-learning projects will have a successful outcome, you probably don't want to assign mission-critical projects here. If a project is truly mission-critical, the company should assign people whose capabilities have already been proven to solve the challenge. In this latter case, you might consider assigning one or more of the Hi-Pos to the task force or committee that will take responsibility for the project, using this as an experiential learning opportunity.

Tying Projects to Educational Topics

The purpose of the assigned action-learning projects is to help the LDP participants use what they have learned in the classroom, thereby reinforcing learning and helping to ensure that what is learned will be applied to participants' work. This tie-in is critical, but it is not always easy to accomplish.

Start by collecting ideas for action-learning projects from as many sources within the company as possible, starting with the company's executives (there is no better way of ensuring continuing executive support for the LDP than to demonstrate that the program is helping them solve some of their long-standing challenges). What are the challenges facing the company? What are some of the long-standing issues that, while not mission-critical, would benefit the company if they could be resolved? What are some "nice-to-haves"—things that the company wishes it could do but has never had the time or manpower to accomplish? Develop as long a list of potential projects as possible *before* the LDP begins so that you can give participants some choices.

You can also discuss the action-learning projects with the program faculty you will be using. In their experience, what kinds of action-learning

====

Analyzing Company Performance

The company's new CEO and CFO started a new tradition of quarterly all-employee teleconferences immediately after the release of each quarter's results. They also started including a number of performance measures in their presentations, both for their own company as well as for several direct competitors and other companies of the same size in other industries. Most employees had never seen these types of performance measures, had no idea what they meant, and basically ignored them.

With the next LDP education session focusing on financial analysis, the CFO stepped up to help. With a business simulation being used for the first two days of the program to help participants better understand how income statements and balance sheets were generated and how to read financial statements, the CFO came in to do the last half-day session himself. He explained the various performance measures that he and the CEO included in the quarterly presentations, explained why they were important, and demonstrated how they were derived from public sources of information. He then assigned an action-learning project to each of the participants (each participant was given the name of a company, either a direct competitor or a company of similar size in a similar industry) to derive the quarterly performance measures for that company for the past two years.

At the start of the next education session (three months later), each participant reported the findings and the CFO had all of the data collated into one big report. The CFO and the CEO were both elated by the results: They now had 36 well-regarded mid-level managers from every business unit, geographic area, and functional group who understood what the numbers meant and why they were important and who could explain them to their colleagues and employees.

====

projects can best help the participants apply what they will learn in the session? What types of projects have arisen from the educational sessions that the faculty have given in other companies?

Assigning or Selecting Projects

There are times when you will want to assign specific action-learning projects to the LDP participants and other times when you want to give them guidelines for projects and then let them define the projects themselves. In the sidebar, where the CFO wanted the participants to generate performance measurements for a list of specific companies, each participant was assigned a specific company to analyze.

Similarly, there may be specific areas of opportunity that have been challenging executives for years that they would like the groups within the LDP to tackle. In these cases, the optimal strategy is to have the specified executives present the challenges to the participants, explain why they are important, and tell participants what types of results they would like to see. They should not impose solutions—if they had the solutions, they wouldn't need the participants' help—but should let the participants use their own ingenuity to determine how best to tackle each challenge.

Other benefits can arise from letting participants select their own projects:

- Having an active brainstorming session to generate project ideas as part of the educational session can spark enthusiasm among the participants. At the same time, by using a skilled facilitator, the participants can learn how to run a formal brainstorming session—a skill that can prove useful in their regular jobs.
- When participants define their own action-learning projects, they feel more ownership for the projects and the results of those projects than if they are assigned a specific task by someone else.
- Because all of the participants are Hi-Pos, allowing them to use their own ingenuity to define action-learning projects may well result in better, more interesting, and more impactful projects than those that might have been defined by one or two other people and then imposed on them.

The considerations on assigning specific projects or letting LDP participants choose their own projects are summarized in table 4-1.

Structuring Action-Learning Projects

A suggested form for describing action-learning projects is presented in worksheet 4-1. Require LDP participants to complete this form within one week of each educational session and submit it to the LDP manager.

How to Better Engage Employees

The company had not been doing well for the past few years. There had been several rounds of reductions in force, unpaid furloughs, no salary increases or bonuses, and lower stock prices, which had put most employees' stock options under water. A lot of employees, including many of the LDP participants, had their résumés out on the street and on the Internet, and the company was losing some key people to competitors.

The LDP education session for this quarter was led by Jim Clemmer, a leadership consultant from Canada. He described how employees react to "stormy seas." "Some people act as navigators," he said, "some like survivors, and some like victims." It was a powerful message. A number of the participants remarked that before the session, they thought that they had been acting as navigators, but in the face of Clemmer's presentation, they realized that they were acting more like victims, and they vowed to change their behavior.

For the action-learning projects following this education session, the CEO and the senior vice president of HR presented the challenge. Because all in the group were designated as having high potential for future leadership roles in the company, now was the time to start demonstrating some of that leadership. The company's employees were badly disengaged. The assignment for each of the six teams of participants was to create a project that would start re-engaging employees. The projects did not have to cover the entire employee population, but could be pilot efforts that, if successful, could be replicated with other groups around the company.

Most of the teams stepped up to the challenge very well. One team created a General Electric–style workout session that helped employees solve some problems that had been frustrating them for a long time. Another team used a video camera to interview enthusiastic employees about how much they liked working for the company and the types of interesting work they did to create a video called "We are [company name]." While the video was not professional enough to use as is, the marketing communications group followed up to do it more professionally, and the tape became an excellent tool for college recruitment.

Table 4-1. Action-learning projects.

Methods Used	Challenges Well-Defined	Challenges Not Well-Defined
Assigned	Specific projects assigned to LDP participants or teams Example: Performance analysis of selected companies	Challenge statement broadly defined, but specific methods and tools must be used Example: Reengineer a business process
Open, but given parameters	Well-defined assignment, but methods open Example: Personal vision statements	General topic assigned, but methods and specific project left to participants Example: Employee engagement

Components of the description for each action-learning project include the following:

- a title for the action-learning project
- objectives for the action-learning project
- due date (prior to the next education session)
- description of the project (what the individual or team plans to do)
- names of executive sponsor or assigned coach (if applicable)
- names of team leader and other team members (if applicable)
- optimal outcomes (expected accomplishments through the project).

Other Considerations

What else do you need to consider in planning action-learning projects for your LDP? Here are a few other things to consider:

- whether to use individual or team projects
- whether to assign a coach to projects
- how participants will report on their projects
- how to debrief participants on their projects
- how to measure performance on the projects.

Worksheet 4-1. Action-learning project description.

Project Title: _____

Objectives:

- _____
- _____
- _____

Due Date:_____

Description:

_____
_____
_____
_____

Sponsor:_____

Coach: _____

Team:
- Leader:_____
- Members:_____

_____
_____
_____

Optimal Outcomes:

- _____
- _____
- _____

Notes:

_____
_____
_____
_____

Individual Versus Team Projects

Over the course of the entire LDP, you may choose to have some individual projects and some team projects. Chapter 3 recommends that the first action-learning project focus on each individual creating a personal vision statement. While this suggests individual work, assign the participants to teams for this project. By assigning participants to teams, they can help each other through discussions and reviews, at the same time getting to know each other better and starting to build their personal relationships. The results may be not only better vision statements, but also a stronger team relationship that will yield benefits on future team projects.

The teams themselves should be constituted to have as broad a span of business units, functional areas, and geographies as possible. In this way, team members will learn more about each other's parts of the business as they work together. While it may seem simpler to put all of the people from Asia together and all the engineering managers together, the point of assigning teams is to help participants work across geographic, functional, and time barriers.

Once teams are formed, it is recommended to keep the teams intact for a series of three or four projects. This strategy enables the team members to build their relationships over time and determine how they can best work together on the various projects. You will see improved team functioning as you move from project to project. And, when you later assign projects to individuals, you will see that the former teammates continue to help and support each other.

Work with your company's IT department to set up a set of tools that LDP participants can use to facilitate their communication and teamwork. These tools might include teleconferences, web conferences, discussion boards, and wikis. In most companies, many of these tools already exist on the company intranet. There are also a number of tools available for free on the Internet that teams can use, but even if participants want to use these free tools, the company's IT group should be involved in their selection to ensure the privacy of any proprietary information.

Coaches

As will be discussed at greater length in chapter 8, the company's HR group should be actively involved in the selection of LDP participants and in providing ongoing guidance to those participants. Each LDP participant should know which HR professional will be his or her resource person throughout the program. For individual projects, it can only help to have these HR professionals check in periodically with their assigned participants on how they are progressing. For team projects, you may want to assign an HR person or another subject matter expert (depending on the topic of the action-learning project) to periodically check in with each team to ensure that the project plan is on track. If there is a project sponsor, for example, the CFO for the performance reporting example presented earlier, this sponsor can also act as a coach.

Informal coaching can also help identify any roadblocks that arise and offer assistance to get a team unstuck if necessary. Further coaching from the education session faculty can also be undertaken through virtual follow-up sessions as described in chapter 3.

Project Reporting

A key feature of the LDP model is to have participants report the results of their action-learning projects to an executive review panel at the start of the next education session. For the participants, this sends an important message that the projects are important and that their performance on the projects is going to be very visible. For the executives who serve on the panel, these presentations provide an opportunity to view participants who are not normally in their line of sight and to start forming impressions about the participants' capabilities for future leadership roles in the company.

Select the panel from among company executives and in general limit it to four to six people. You can vary the composition of the panel each time to maximize the number of executives involved throughout the LDP. If an education session is being held at one particular location, such as at the company's European headquarters, invite members of the local management team to be part of the panel.

The review session should be moderated by the LDP manager, who will facilitate the presentations and the interaction between the participants and the panel. Each individual or team can have six to 10 minutes to make a presentation that follows the outline of the action-learning project report, as shown in worksheet 4-2. The panel members will then spend a few minutes asking questions or making comments on the project. With team projects, it is up to the team to decide who will present to the panel, although it is recommended that all team members participate in the presentation. With individual projects, you may need to divide into more than one room so that there is sufficient time to handle all presentations.

The project reports and the interactions with the executive review panel will be collected and made part of each participant's record (as will be discussed at greater length in chapter 7).

This format includes the basic project information taken from the original project description, but also includes project outcomes, discussion of problems and challenges encountered and how they were handled, and the individual's or team's recommendation on any follow-through items that may have arisen. For example, this latter section may describe a successful pilot project and provide recommendations on how to broaden the project beyond the pilot stage.

Plan to submit this report to the LDP manager at least one week prior to the next education session. The LDP manager will then make copies of the reports for the members of the executive review panel prior to the start of the education session. The format for reporting on projects at that session will be discussed shortly.

Participant Debriefings

While the participants will present the results of their action-learning projects to an executive review panel at the start of the next education session, they also need to be debriefed about the experience. This reflection on their projects and dialogue around it with other team members and their HR representative or coach is a method of taking their newly developed knowledge (gained by applying what they learned in

Worksheet 4-2. Action-learning project report.

Project Title: _____

Objectives:

- _____
- _____
- _____

Due Date:_____

Description:

_____
_____
_____
_____

Sponsor:_____

Coach: _____

Team:

- Leader:_____
- Members:_____

  _____
  _____
  _____

Outcomes:

- _____
- _____
- _____

Problems/Challenges Encountered and How They Were Handled:

- _____
- _____
- _____

Follow-Through and Recommendations:

How will your work on this action-learning project continue beyond the end of the project? What recommendations would you make to other LDP participants and to the company based on the results of your project?

_____
_____
_____
_____

the last education session) and moving on to Stage IV of the learning model—wisdom.

The ideal way of conducting this debriefing is with the assistance of their assigned HR person or project coach. Debriefing can also become part of each participant's personal learning journal, as will be described in chapter 5.

Questions to be included in the debriefing session include the following:

- How successful do you believe you were with this project?
- How could you have made it more successful?
- What stood in your way to achieving optimal results?
- How could you have overcome any obstacles you encountered?
- If you were to start the project anew, knowing what you know now, what would you do differently?
- What have you learned from the experience?
- How can you apply what you have learned to your current job?
- What will you remember from the experience as you move up the management/leadership ladder?

Performance Measurements

In measuring performance on action-learning projects, be concerned not just with what was actually accomplished but even more with what the participants learned through the experience. From the project reports and the presentations that will be made to the executive review panel, it will be clear that some projects were more successful than others and, in fact, some may have failed totally. You need to remember that the primary purpose of action-learning projects is to help participants apply what they have learned in the education sessions, so your basic evaluation measure is whether this happened.

At the same time, remember that the action-learning projects are designed to give the company's current leaders an opportunity to observe this group of Hi-Pos and to test their leadership abilities. Thus, even if a project is very successful in terms of meeting its original objectives, you also want to observe other factors:

- Who stepped up to lead the team?
- How well did each individual work as part of the team?
- How well did the participants work with people outside the LDP to accomplish their project's objectives?
- Did the participants use the project to accomplish their personal learning goals, or did they just get it done to satisfy the requirement?
- Who saw the longer-term implications of what they accomplished and stepped up to create a longer-term plan for implementation beyond the scope of the project itself?

Whether an individual or team had a wildly successful project or failed badly, this is vital information that can be used to judge the readiness of LDP participants for future leadership positions.

Summary

The action-learning projects described in this chapter together with the LDP education sessions form the core of the LDP. Action-learning projects help participants apply what they have learned, thereby assisting in the transformation of information into personal knowledge. The action-learning projects also provide opportunities to test the leadership capabilities of LDP participants *before* making promotional decisions, thereby helping the company to avoid costly promotional errors.

Experiential learning can also be a valuable tool to broaden participants' understanding of the company's business. Experiential learning can be incorporated into the overall LDP plan or can be part of IDPs.

The combination of education sessions and action-learning projects is designed for the entire LDP audience. But each LDP participant will also have individual areas for development that cannot always be addressed with the overall group. For this reason, the third part of the LDP model is individual assessment and the creation of an IDP for each participant, as will be discussed in chapter 5.

Chapter 5

LDP Individual Development Plans and Guidance

What's In This Chapter

- What is a 360-degree assessment?
- How are 360-degree assessments used to build on individual strengths?
- How are individual development plans written?
- How are individual development plans used in the LDP?
- What is a learning contract, and how is it used?
- How can LDP participants use personal learning journals to guide their own development?

E very individual in your company's pool of high-potentials is unique— each with educational and work backgrounds, each with a series of personal accomplishments within and without your company, each with areas of strength and areas that would benefit from further development. While the overall leadership development program agenda can help build a common set of competencies for the entire group, each participant will benefit greatly from individual guidance and from an individual development plan that complements the LDP agenda.

This chapter will focus on these individual development needs. To assess individual differences in development needs, start by doing a 360-degree assessment of each Hi-Po in your LDP group. With the data from the 360-degree review and other information you have gathered in the process of selecting your Hi-Pos, create an IDP for each LDP participant in the form of a learning contract that will complement and supplement the LDP agenda. Finally, this chapter will discuss the option of asking LDP participants to keep personal learning journals that will help them focus on what they have learned throughout the entire program.

360-Degree Assessments

A 360-degree assessment is a survey that provides a number of questions and a rating scale on a variety of competencies related to how well the individual knows and manages him- or herself, knows and manages other people, and knows and manages the business. It differs from a performance evaluation in that the individual is rated by

- him- or herself
- manager
- several peers
- several employees.

This gives a more complete (or 360-degree) view of the individual and can be very helpful in discovering both areas of strength and areas needing development. Please note that this is an *assessment* rather than an evaluation. Its purpose is developmental, not judgmental. The 360-degree assessment will serve as the foundation of discussions on which the IDP will be based. As will be discussed in chapter 7, the LDP participants may take other types of assessments as part of the LDP, and these can also provide useful information for the IDPs.

Plan to do the 360-degree assessments after the second or third LDP education session. The reason for waiting until then, rather than starting the LDP process with these assessments, is to give participants time to develop a degree of comfort with the overall program. You can then explain that the 360-degree assessment will be part of a process to write an IDP for each LDP participant. Also, because the participants will have had the benefit of the first session that speaks to leadership characteristics, they will be better able to understand the results of the 360-degree assessment and the importance of each item in it.

There are dozens of vendors of 360-degree assessments in the marketplace. Many have assessment instruments that they have been using and refining for years, while others will offer to create a customized assessment just for your company and your purposes. How do you choose between those options?

Packaged Assessments Versus Customized Assessments

Any 360-degree assessment you use should reflect the core competencies that your company has determined are most important for its future leaders, as discussed in chapter 1. At the same time, there are no secret or magic competencies that your company will put on its list that don't exist elsewhere. So, while a packaged assessment may include more items than you have on your list, or may phrase some competencies differently than you would, all of these assessment instruments are generally alike. Some may be based on the assessment company's own competency model while others use the phrasing made popular by the company founder's book on leadership competencies, but they will all yield roughly the same information.

The advantages of using a long-standing 360-degree assessment are as follows:

- The questions are more likely to have been tested for statistical reliability and validity.
- The company may have a historical database that can be used to compare your Hi-Pos with their peers from similar companies or industries.
- Because of the historical database, the data collected may be subject to richer interpretation by the vendor.

- Because the assessment company has used the same questions for so long, they may have an excellent guide for interpreting the assessment results.
- Because the assessment instruments and the processes for administering the instruments have been in place for so long, the costs for doing the assessment may be lower than for a customized assessment.

There are also some disadvantages to using canned assessments:

- Some assessment companies have so much historical data that they produce reports that are so lengthy that the people using the reports find them burdensome. Some reports run 200 or more pages including 50 or more pages of colorful graphs that are of limited usefulness.
- Sometimes the reports are so complicated that the assessment company will insist that you hire its consultants to debrief the participants, and this can become very costly.
- There are times when you do want to customize the 360-degree assessment instrument. For example, you may want to include some items about the individual's understanding of your company's business processes and core technologies.

There are also many assessment companies that will customize the instrument however you want. This allows you to focus on what your company considers the key competencies for your future leaders. This also tends to make the reports coming from the assessments more manageable in length. But there are also disadvantages to using a customized 360-degree assessment:

- By using a customized 360-degree assessment, you lose the benefit of using the assessment company's historical database to compare your employees with their peers from other companies and industries.
- There will be additional fees charged to customize your assessment instrument.
- The interpretation guides often offered by the assessment company may not fit with the assessment questions you have selected.

Vendor Selection

While it is certainly possible for your company to create and administer its own 360-degree assessment instrument, it is probably better that you use one of the many vendors that offer these types of instruments. Especially in the small to mid-sized company, your staff probably doesn't have the capacity to do it all in-house, and the costs of using an external vendor are generally reasonable.

When you do decide to conduct these assessments, there are a number of things you should consider in selecting a vendor:

- *Should you use stock or customized assessments?* Will you use the vendor's stock 360-degree assessment or ask the vendor to customize it for your purposes? A customized version will generally be more expensive than a stock version. Many 360-degree assessment vendors will be happy to use their stock version and add on a few items specific to your company at little extra cost.

- *Is the instrument reliable and valid?* The better assessment companies have psychometricians on staff who have tested the instruments and the individual assessment items for statistical reliability and validity. Make certain that the vendor you choose has done this type of testing.

- *How useful are the generated reports?* Some companies try to awe you with the size of the reports they generate. Request a sample report from the vendor (often available on the vendor's website) to judge how easy it will be for you and your colleagues to use.

- *Does the vendor provide a debriefing guide?* Some, but not all, vendors have written useful debriefing guides to help you interpret the results of the assessment. Get a copy and read it. How helpful will it be?

- *Does the vendor provide debriefing services or training on how to debrief the assessment reports?* Many of the larger vendors offer services where they will send in their own consultants to debrief each individual report. Others may offer training for your HR staff on how to interpret and debrief the assessment report. Obviously, using the vendor's consultants will be more expensive than training your own. Determine how much you are willing to spend and whether the additional expense of using the vendor's consultants is worth it to you. Also, don't forget to check with references to get feedback on the quality of the debriefings provided by the vendor's consultants or the quality of the training they provided to the customer's internal staff.

- *Does the vendor provide administration services?* Many vendors have the systems and personnel in place to administer the assessments from start to finish. That is, you provide for each individual the name and contact information for each person's assessors, and the vendor handles the distribution of the instruments, the follow-ups and reminders, the collection, and the processing of the assessments. This can remove a large burden from your internal staff. Ask whether the administration process is included in the fees.

Some Cautions

There are a few things to watch out for in administering 360-degree assessments:

- First, you have to establish an atmosphere of trust with those being assessed—otherwise, they will not cooperate and will be skeptical of the results. This is another reason why you should wait until after the second or third LDP education session to administer the assessments—it gives participants time to build trust in the overall program.
- Second, make it clear to both the participants and the assessors that what they put on the instruments is absolutely confidential and will only be presented as a statistical aggregate. If your company has trust issues, or if participants have trust issues with employees or managers, assessors, fearing that their responses will be seen by the participants and attributed directly to them, may not be as candid in their assessments as you would like.
- Third, while the assessment is not designed to be a measure of performance, you can use it to measure participants' progress on various leadership competencies by administering the same

assessment again at the end of the LDP, that is, 12 to 18 months after the first administration. This second view (sometimes called a 720-degree assessment, because it repeats the 360-degree assessment) can point out the areas where each participant has made progress and where there is still progress to be made.

What You See ISN'T What You Get

When we decided to do 360-degree assessments on the company's top 50 managers, we knew that there were trust issues among the company's leadership that trickled down to all levels. Would the assessors be candid on the instruments, or would they be less than candid, fearing that, despite pledges of confidentiality, the people they were rating would see their ratings? We decided to test the level of candor by interviewing the assessors after they had completed the written assessments. The results were astounding!

What we heard from the interviews was, in many cases, totally different from what we saw in the statistical ratings. And yes, the reason for this was that the assessors feared retribution from their managers or their peers.

You cannot make people trust you or the system. But, if you fear that a lack of trust in the organization will skew the assessment results, you should plan to follow up the written assessments with interviews of the assessors to ensure that you are getting the full picture.

Once you have selected a vendor and administered the 360-degree assessments, the next step is to create an IDP for each LDP participant.

Individual Development Plans

It is important to have a plan for debriefing the results of the 360-degree assessment with the employee. As discussed in the section on selecting a 360-degree assessment vendor, the debriefing can be done by the vendor's personnel or by your own HR staff. If you use the vendor's staff to debrief the assessment, the HR staff member assigned to the Hi-Po should be included in the meeting. If you choose to do the debriefing with your own HR staff, you can conduct training (typically provided by the 360-degree vendor) for your staff before starting.

The initial debrief meeting should include the employee, the HR staff member, and, if applicable, the vendor's consultant. Later, you will include the employee's manager and sometimes the employee's mentor in the discussion of the IDP. The reason for excluding the manager and the mentor from this initial meeting is to be able to hold a frank discussion of the results without embarrassing the employee and to give the employee time to digest the results before holding the development discussion with the manager.

There will typically be some surprises in the 360-degree assessment results. There may be areas that the employees feel are particular strengths, but which the other assessors saw as weaknesses. There may be areas of strength identified by the other assessors that the employees never felt were particular areas of strength. What you are going to uncover with the results are areas of competence and incompetence, some of which are conscious for the employee and some of which are unconscious, as shown in the matrix in table 5-1:

- Areas of conscious competence are those where the employees know what they know: "I'm good at this, and I know it."
- Areas of conscious incompetence are those where the employees lack knowledge or skills and know that they need to develop: "I know that I am weak in that area."
- Areas of unconscious competence are those where others recognize that the employees have skills or knowledge, but the employees haven't recognized this strength. Often, natural leaders have skills that they do not recognize themselves, but that others have noted.
- Areas of unconscious incompetence are those where the employees lack knowledge or skills, but are unaware of this deficit.

The discussion with the employee should debrief the 360-degree assessment results and give the employee an opportunity to reflect and comment on the findings. After the debrief, organize a larger meeting where the results of the assessment can be brought together with past performance reviews, the employee's personal vision statement, and the input of the employee's manager and mentor to discuss the employee's strengths, the areas needing development, and what should go

Table 5-1. Areas of competence and incompetence.

	Competence	Incompetence
Conscious	**Conscious Competence:** I know what I know	**Conscious Incompetence:** I know what I don't know
Unconscious	**Unconscious Competence:** I am unaware that I know something	**Unconscious Incompetence:** I don't know what I don't know

into the employee's IDP. In this meeting, you will discuss the employee's strengths and the areas where the employee needs to develop further.

The responsibility for employee development belongs primarily to the employee. In creating the IDP, there are several people who need to be involved and several sources of information to use. Creating the IDP is generally led by an HR staff member working with the employee and the employee's direct manager. If your LDP model includes the assignment of a mentor to each LDP participant, the mentor can also play a role in creating the IDP.

The process starts with debriefing and reviewing the 360-degree assessment and any other assessments that the employee has completed as part of the LDP education process. This will give the HR staff member, the employee, and the manager an overview of areas of employee strength and areas that need strengthening.

You may also review the employee's personal vision statement if it was written as part of the LDP (remember that this was the recommended action-learning project to be completed between the first and second LDP education sessions). From these two inputs, there can be an open discussion of the following:

- employee's career ambitions
- employee's strengths to help achieve ambitions
- developmental activities to supplement the LDP content.

Employee's Career Ambitions

What does the employee see in the future? To what level of the organization does the employee aspire? After learning through the LDP what it will take to become a leader in the company, some employees may decide that they are not willing to make the investment in themselves that will be required to eventually achieve an executive leadership position. They may decide that they are very happy managing an engineering group or a marketing group without ever becoming vice president of the function. A salesperson may decide that his or her real rewards come from working directly with customers and that he or she has no ambition to become a sales manager. Some may decide to follow a technical leadership career path rather than a managerial leadership career path, becoming more expert in the domain of their technical expertise and providing leadership within their technical specialty rather than managing people and budgets. All of these considerations will have a major bearing on the employee's development plan.

Employee's Strengths to Help Achieve Ambitions

From the 360-degree assessment and any other assessments the employee has completed as part of the LDP, there will be a number of areas of strength that have been identified. How well do these strengths fit in with the employee's career ambitions? For example, if technical expertise is identified as a strength, this competency may fit better with a technical career path more than with a managerial career path, or a strength in business acumen can prove more useful for a general management role than a technical role.

It is easier to build on an employee's strengths than it is to overcome weak areas. In their book, *Smarts: Are We Hard-Wired for Success?*, Chuck Martin and his colleagues (2007) argue that people's brains are hard-wired in certain ways and that it is not always possible to overcome that wiring. For example, if you have a messy, unorganized office, it may be that your brain is not wired to allow for organization and neatness. So, no matter how many workshops you take on organizational skills, you are unlikely to greatly and permanently improve your performance on this measure. At the same time, if you are hard-wired to be very organized, this competency can be very useful in certain career paths (for example, to head up a project management office).

Developmental Activities to Supplement the LDP Agenda

The assessments will also point out areas that are in need of further development for the employees to achieve their career ambitions. Some of those areas may be less likely to respond to developmental activities than others due to the nature of the employees' hard-wiring. In those cases, you will discuss how to compensate for those weak areas, rather than to overcome them. For example, in one company, there was a senior manager who, because of learning disabilities, was an incredibly poor speller. He was a brilliant man and an outstanding manager and leader, but it was an embarrassment to him and to the company to have him send out anything written. To compensate for this weakness, the company hired an assistant for him who took dictation and wrote all of his emails, letters, and documents. While this is in stark contrast to the trends of the past few decades that have had employees at all levels typing their own emails and documents on their personal computers, it was the right solution for this person and for the company—the man was a valuable asset and this was the way to ensure his continuing value to the company.

For those areas needing development that are not going to be covered by the LDP agenda, you should create a plan for how to achieve those learning goals. The plan may include sending the employee to internal or external training, a program of self-study, or changes in job roles or assignments to help the employee develop. In planning the employee's personal learning agenda, it can be useful to include the employee's mentor (if you have built a mentoring component into the LDP model), because the mentor can suggest and often has the power to place the employee in some learning situations where the employee and manager do not. For example, the mentor might suggest that the employee join a cross-functional task force to get exposure to other parts of the business or might suggest that the employee take a six-month overseas assignment to fill in for a manager in another country who is going on maternity leave. The mentor, because of the higher-level position in the company, may have more knowledge of these opportunities and, just as important, may have the power to arrange for the assignment.

Learning Contracts

An effective way of writing an IDP is to put it in the form of a learning contract that ties the learning need to specific company, group, and individual goals; specifies what learning will take place and by what means; and then specifies both how learning will be applied to the learner's job and what changes in business results are expected from this. The learning contract thus builds in Kirkpatrick's Level 3 and Level 4 evaluations from the start.

A learning contract has three sections:

1. determining the learning need
2. setting the learning agenda
3. applying learning to the job.

The most important thing to remember about building a learning contract is that the contract is completed *before any learning activity begins.* Exhibit 5-1 summarizes the questions that make up a learning contract, as will be discussed below.

Determining the Learning Need

The learning contract always starts with the company's business goals. Once you understand those goals, you need to cascade those goals down to the level of the work group and to the individual for whom you are creating the learning contract, because it is vital to understand how the employee's work contributes to the achievement of individual, team, and company goals.

Once you understand this, you need to ask: "To meet those goals, what needs to change? What needs to be done differently?" When you understand what needs to change or be done differently, you next ask: "To make these changes, what does the employee need to learn?"

Exhibit 5-1. Learning contract questionnaire.

Part I: Determining Learning Needs

1. What are the company's business goals?
2. How do these goals cascade down to the work group and the individual, i.e., how can the employee's work contribute to the achievement of those goals?
3. To meet those goals, what needs to change?
4. Of the things that need to change, which require learning on the part of the employee?
5. What does the employee need to learn?

Part II: Setting the Learning Agenda

1. What are the priorities among the employee's identified learning needs?
2. What sources of learning are available to the employee (training, self-study, on-the-job training, apprenticeship, coaching)?
3. What is the schedule for these learning activities?
4. How will you measure learning achievement?

Part III: Applying Learning to the Job

1. How will the employee apply what was learned to the job?
2. What reinforcement or assistance will be available to the employee to help in this application?
3. What changes in individual, team, and company business results are expected from this application?

It is important to recognize that what needs to change will not always lead you to a learning need. If manufacturing quality is below standard, the changes needed to fix the problem may have to do with the machinery being used or the quality of materials coming from suppliers, rather than from a lack of knowledge or skill on the part of the employee. Companies have wasted untold amounts of money on training to fix problems whose solutions weren't training!

Assuming that the needed changes do require some learning on the part of the individual, this first part of the learning contract will result in the identification of the learning needs.

Setting the Learning Agenda

Once you have determined what needs to be learned, you need to establish how the learning will be achieved. Will the learning needs be met by the LDP agenda? If not, are there other internal or external trainings that will satisfy this learning requirement? Can the learning best be accomplished by on-the-job training or by apprenticing the employee to a subject matter expert for a period of time? Will a new job assignment, permanent or temporary, help the employee meet these learning requirements? Can you find an internal or external coach to help the employee master the needed knowledge or skills?

Once you have answered these questions, you can set the learning agenda to answer the following questions:

- What learning activities are planned?
- What sources (training, self-study, coaching, job assignment) will you use to help the employee learn?
- What is the schedule for the learning to take place?
- What are the priorities among the learning needs identified?
- How long should the required learning take to accomplish?
- How will you measure learning achievement? (This will be discussed in chapter 7.)

Applying Learning to the Job

Learning will yield little or no benefit to the individual or to the company if it isn't applied to the employee's work to make a positive difference in business results. This part of the learning contract specifies, from the start, how learning will be applied to the employee's work and what changes in individual, team, and company business results are expected from this. This section of the learning contract answers these questions:

- *How will learning be applied to the employee's work?* This has to be part of the plan from the beginning. People will pay more attention to what they are learning if they know that there is an expectation that they will immediately apply their learning to their work.
- *What reinforcement or assistance will the employee need to apply this learning?* Just as you are building reinforcement into the LDP education

sessions, you need to ensure that the employees know where or to whom to go if they need assistance to apply what was learned. This may require help from the employees' managers, from another employee who has already mastered the knowledge or skill, or from the learning instructor. Sometimes, you can send two or more people from the group to the same learning event so that they can reinforce and help each other with application.

- *What changes in individual, team, or company performance do you expect to result from this application?* This ties the learning back to the first part of the learning contract. In Part I, you specified the individual, team, and company goals that needed to be achieved, and then determined what needed to change to meet those goals. If your learning agenda has been properly planned, this measurement was specified in Part I. Here, you need to specify how the results will be measured in terms of individual, team, or company performance against those goals. A primary tenet of program evaluation is that a properly written objective will yield its own measurement.

Table 5-2 summarizes the three sections of the learning contract.

Personal Learning Journals

Even though you are helping your company's Hi-Pos develop their leadership competencies through the LDP by means of 360-degree assessments and IDPs and, as will be discussed in chapter 6, through mentoring and coaching, the primary responsibility for each employee's development remains with that employee.

Table 5-2. The learning contract.

Learning Contract Section	Yields
Part I: Determining Learning Needs	Prioritized list of learning needs
Part II: Setting the Learning Agenda	Learning plan
Part III: Applying Learning to the Job	Action plan and evaluation measures

Looking back to the four stages of learning, the development of knowledge comes from applying learning to the job and the development of wisdom comes from reflection, discussion, and dialogue on the employee's experiences in making these applications. For this reason, each LDP participant should be encouraged to write a personal learning journal.

The personal learning journal can help the employees keep track of what they have learned in the LDP education sessions, through the action-learning projects, and from applying what they have learned to their work. Entries in the journal might include the following:

- *Notes from each LDP education session.* What do the employees consider most important from the LDP education sessions? What did the employees learn? Similar notes can be made for any non-LDP trainings that the employees attend, from books and articles they read, from trade shows or conventions attended, or from conversations with their managers or others.
- *Debriefing notes from action-learning projects.* What worked and what didn't? What would the employees do differently if they were to start again from scratch? What have they learned as they observed other LDP participants and listened to their reports on their action-learning projects?
- *Observations from the 360-degree assessment.* What surprised the employees the most? What strengths were identified? What weaknesses? Were there areas that the employees thought were strengths but others identified as areas for development?
- *Insights from mentor.* What lessons have employees learned from their mentors? What has arisen in the course of the LDP or on their regular jobs that the employees would like to discuss with their mentors?

Many LDP participants who have started personal learning journals for the program have found it so personally valuable that they have continued the journal past the end of the LDP.

The writing of a personal learning journal is a costless option for your LDP, but it can be of great assistance to the participants if they take it seriously and use it. Finally, the personal learning journal is by definition *personal*—there should never be a requirement to share it with anyone else.

Summary

The third element of the LDP model is individual guidance and the writing of an IDP for each LDP participant. Each Hi-Po in your LDP group will have a unique set of accomplishments, education, and personal characteristics, and you need to pay heed to these to develop each individual to his or her greatest potential. A 360-degree assessment starts the individual assessment that leads to the IDP, which specifies learning activities to be undertaken to complement and supplement the LDP agenda. The IDP should take the form of a learning contract that ties learning to specific individual, team, and company business objectives and, from the start, sets expectations for the application of learning to the individual's work and the business results that should ensue. The learning methods specified within the IDP may include formal learning activities as well as experiential learning. Coaching and mentoring may also be included in the IDP—these two learning methods are the subject of the next chapter.

Chapter 6

LDP Mentoring, Coaching, and Reinforcement

What's In This Chapter

- What role does mentoring play in the LDP model?
- How do you prepare mentors and mentoring clients?
- What role do internal and external coaches play in the LDP model?
- How do you select mentors and coaches for the LDP participants?

The fourth major element of the leadership development program model is mentoring, coaching, and reinforcement. While these three elements may suggest some overlap, there are distinct ways of setting up each as an effective learning method. This chapter discusses how you can set up a mentoring program for LDP participants and how you should train the mentors, the mentoring clients (or mentees), and the managers of the mentoring clients. It will also discuss the use of coaching within the LDP and a variety of methods of reinforcing the participants' learning back on their jobs.

Mentoring

A mentor is a wise and trusted counselor or teacher. For the purposes of the LDP model, this book recommends that each of the participants be assigned a mentor from the company's senior executive staff. Here are some guidelines for appointing mentors for your group of high-potentials:

- Mentors should be at least two levels above the mentoring clients in the organization and be part of a different reporting structure within the organization. That is, a mentor shouldn't be the employee's manager's manager. One reason for this is so that the mentors can broaden the employees' views of the organization and the industry, including history, culture, and norms of behavior. Another reason is to broaden the mentors' views of organizational talent outside their own part of the organization.

- Mentors should be well respected within the organization and have distinguished histories within the company or the industry. Not every executive should automatically be placed as a mentor. A mentor must establish a climate of mutual trust and respect with the mentoring client and be willing to take the time to play the role of a mentor. If executives state that they do not want to be mentors, you should not force the assignment. Someone who doesn't want to play the role will most likely not do a good job.

- The mentor should be placed highly enough within the organization to know of developmental opportunities that may not be directly visible to the employee or the employee's manager and to have the ability to make or directly influence the appointment of the employee to those opportunities. This is not to say that the mentor will make these decisions without the input of the employee's manager, but that the mentor can advise the employee and the manager of appropriate opportunities as they arise.

- You need to provide training to mentors on their role in the LDP, as will be discussed later in this chapter.

Mentoring Relationships

Mentoring relationships among the mentor, the mentoring client, and the client's direct manager can be confusing and can create conflict if the roles are not well defined. Therefore, it is important that all members of the mentoring program (the mentor, the mentoring client, and the mentoring client's manager) know their purpose.

The Role of the Mentor

The role of the mentor is to provide education and career guidance to the mentoring client. For example, a senior editor in the publishing industry related how, when he was a junior editor at a major publishing house, he was assigned a senior vice president as his mentor who took him to lunch once a month for his first year on the job. He said that over the course of a year, he learned more about the publishing industry and about how the company worked than he could have on his own in 10 years.

The mentor is also there to dispense advice. For example, the mentor may advise on career paths within the company or may help the mentoring client network with other people inside and outside the company who can help the mentoring client's education. A key point here is that the mentoring client must have the choice to take the advice or not. According to Don Blohowiak of Leadwell, who has trained many mentors and mentoring clients in a variety of companies, it is not the mentor's role to force the mentoring client into the mentor's point of view. The role of the mentor should be to help the mentoring client question assumptions—to act as an adviser and a thinking partner.

Finally, the mentor can make suggestions on learning activities. For example, if mentors feel that the mentoring clients need to learn more about other parts of the business, they may suggest that mentoring clients serve on cross-functional task forces or take temporary assignments to fill in for someone who is going on medical leave. Because mentors are senior members of the company, they are more likely to know about such opportunities and may have greater influence on making such appointments.

The Role of the Mentoring Client

The mentoring client's role is to learn and to reciprocate. This is not to say that the mentoring client must automatically take every piece of advice offered by the mentor. The key here is that there must be a mutual respect between the mentor and the mentoring client, so that the mentoring client can be grateful for advice given, but may also respectfully decline to take that advice. The mentoring client can also look for ways to reciprocate: Because the mentoring client comes from a different functional area than the mentor, as well as a different educational and experiential background, the mentoring client may also be able to provide some learning to the mentor. Another facet of the respectful mentor–mentoring client relationship is that either party can end the relationship if it doesn't seem to be working.

The key to the success of a mentoring program is to properly set expectations and provide some training to mentors and mentoring clients, as well as to the mentoring clients' direct managers, as discussed below.

The Role of the Mentoring Client's Manager

Often, when a company starts a mentoring program, the managers of the mentoring clients express a number of qualms:

- Does this mean that my employee is now reporting to the mentor rather than to me?
- Is the mentor going to give work assignments to my employee? Will I have a say in what work my employee is assigned to do, or is it being taken out of my hands?
- Who is responsible for my employee's performance review? Me? Or the mentor?
- What if I think the mentor is giving my employee poor advice?
- Are they going to discuss me and second-guess my decisions?

Because these types of questions are so commonly asked by the managers of the mentoring clients, it is a good idea to provide a short (60- to 90-minute) briefing for those managers at the start of the mentoring program. The purpose of the briefing is to explain the program and how it will affect their employees who will be involved in the program and to answer questions, such as those listed above, to calm any fears or anxieties the managers may have about the program. The chances of the mentoring program's success will be improved by briefing these managers so they do not covertly subvert the program because of their fears.

Mentor and Client Training

If the mentoring program you set up as part of the LDP is a new venture for the company, it is appropriate to conduct training sessions for both mentors and mentoring clients. These sessions need only take a few hours. Following is a discussion of what should be covered in each training session.

Mentor Training

The most important part of the orientation of new mentors is for them to understand their role in the process. They are there to serve as advisers and thinking partners; to get the mentoring clients to question their assumptions; and to educate them about the company, its culture and values, and potential career paths. For many senior executives, they will need to change their order-giving habits—they are there to offer advice, not give orders. The mentor must also understand that the mentoring client still has a direct manager who assigns work, evaluates performance, and makes decisions on work assignments and rewards.

The mentor can also be made aware that the mentoring relationship is a two-way street, that is, there will be opportunities for the mentor to learn from the mentoring client. Although the mentor, due to higher rank and more years of experience in the company and the industry, probably has a greater store of knowledge than the mentoring client, the mentoring client has a different set of education and experience that may yield new ideas for the mentor.

Mentors have to be trained on how to give advice, rather than orders. Mentors are there to deal with their clients' agendas, not their own. They generally need to learn that by reflecting on their own experiences with mentoring clients, the mentors may themselves also gain insights into those experiences. In terms of learning, the mentors should consider themselves peers of the mentoring clients.

Ideally, the training session for mentors does not last more than half a day and includes some role-play exercises.

Mentoring Client Training

Mentoring clients need to learn about their role in the mentoring process. While they can look to their mentors as people with a lot of experience and wisdom to share with them, their mentors are not them, and they are not their direct managers. According to Don Blohowiak, a common danger is for the mentoring client to take the mentor's advice as a prescription, but the mentoring clients must remember that only they know what is true for them in their own lives. The mentoring clients also need to be told that if they have a problem with their direct managers they need to settle any disagreements directly with that manager—the mentor's role is not to overrule the direct manager or even to listen to complaints about the manager. Finally, mentoring clients must also learn that the mentoring role is reciprocal. They will get more from the relationship if they also give back to their mentors. While the mentor may have many years more experience and be of much higher rank in the company hierarchy, the mentoring client's education and experience are different, and the mentoring client may be able to offer a different and valuable point of view that may help the mentor.

The training session for mentoring clients should last half a day and include some role-play exercises.

Coaching

Think of a coach as a developmentalist. In too many companies, assigning a coach to a person is almost a death knell—when everything else has been tried, and the person is still failing at the job, company executives say, "Well, let's get him (or her) an external coach. If that doesn't work, we'll have to axe him." This rarely works. But in those companies that view coaching in this way, there is a resistance to assigning and accepting coaches, because coaching implies a last-ditch effort to save someone who will probably not survive.

Benefits

Coaching is an integral part of your leadership development toolbox. Coaching can help LDP participants overcome some limitations and fill in some gaps in their knowledge and skills. It can also help them to think differently than they have in the past, to see themselves and their behaviors through a different set of eyes, to broaden their thinking to encompass new ideas, and to give them more confidence to try out some ideas they may have been storing in their heads for some time—to evolve their own thinking faster. The differences between using coaching for these purposes, instead of other learning methods that are used in the LDP, include the following:

- Coaching is useful when a single participant, rather than the larger group, needs help in one area.
- Coaching can be adapted to the learning style of the individual.
- Coaching can be short-term or long-term, whatever the learning need requires.
- Coaching can come from many sources within and without the company.

Focus on the Needs of a Single Participant

Think of coaching as a tool that can be used in writing an IDP as explained in chapter 5. When individual development needs are determined as part of the IDP, and aren't going to be covered in the larger plan for the LDP, coaching can be an alternative to sending the employee to an internal or external learning program or prescribing a course of self-study.

Coaching can be of particular help when the participants need to view themselves through the eyes of others. For example, have you ever attended a presentation skills seminar where you were videotaped as you made a presentation? If you have been through this type of experience, you know that when you watched the videotape, you saw a lot of flaws in your presentation skills that you never realized were there. Perhaps you inserted too many "ums" as you spoke, or perhaps you spent too much time reading the slides to your audience while you faced the screen rather than your audience.

How well do you run your staff meetings? Do you spend too much time talking at your staff, rather than encouraging their participation in discussions? Do you tend to focus on the inputs from one or two staff members, while others sit and never say a word? Do you encourage others' ideas or just focus on your own? With a coach who attends some of these meetings, you can get a different perspective on how well or poorly you are doing, on what you do well, and where and how you can improve your own performance.

Do you need to master a new set of skills or learn more about a particular subject area? One alternative is to take a course at a local college where you get a survey of the entire field. Another alternative is to find a coach who is an expert in the field and who can coach you on your specific learning needs within that field—it can be a faster and more cost-effective solution.

Sometimes coaching will be the right solution, and sometimes there will be a different learning solution that is better for your situation, but you should keep coaching as one of the tools in your development tool kit.

Adapt to the Learning Style of the Individual

Another benefit of coaching is that it can be adapted to the learning style of the individual. Not everyone learns best in a formal classroom setting or from an e-learning program. There are many ways in which people can acquire the knowledge and skills they need. Coaching provides greater flexibility than most other learning methods.

Adapting Learning to the Style of the Client

Bob was a brilliant engineer from a European country. He called himself Bob because his given name was very difficult to spell and to say. Bob had a very thick accent, and while his knowledge of English was excellent and his writing in English was impeccable, people had a very difficult time understanding him in conversations or when he made presentations.

When Bob was given a new job to head up marketing for the company, I met with him to discuss his learning needs with respect to his new position. I had already done some research and had found several one- to two-week executive education programs on strategic marketing at some leading business schools that I believed could help him get a running start in the new role.

Bob thanked me for my suggestions, but said that attending such a program was not what he wanted and was not the way he learned best. Could I find him a professor from one of those business schools to act as his coach? What he wanted was a reading list and the opportunity to work with the professor to discuss what he was reading, as well as to use the professor as a sounding board for some of his ideas.

With some additional research and phone calls, I identified three candidates for this role and set up interviews for each of them with Bob. He selected one as his coach, and the strategy worked very well for him.

Be Long-Term or Short-Term

While most educational programs you plan will have fixed terms, for example, one or more days, or a half-day a week for six weeks, coaching can be planned to be as short as a single session or as long as needed to meet the learning need of the individual.

Learning Outside the Classroom

Once when I had to write a report, I knew that one of my colleagues was an expert at putting together beautiful charts using a spreadsheet program—something that I did not know how to do, and, at the same time, would benefit me greatly in putting together this report. I asked him to coach me on how to do this. It took about 90 minutes for him to transfer this knowledge to me in sufficient quantity to complete the report. My alternatives would have been to sign up for a three-day program on the spreadsheet software, which would have repeated a lot of what I already knew, or to slog through a manual and try to figure it out myself. This one-time, 90-minute coaching session was exactly what I needed to solve my immediate challenge.

At other times, a coach is needed for a longer term of engagement. When you are trying to introduce a major behavioral change in people, it can take time for them first to recognize the problems with their current behavior and then to learn and practice new behaviors while breaking long-standing habits.

An Action Can Be Worth a Thousand Words

In many ways, Dave was a very successful business unit head—he always made his numbers and his business unit consistently met sales and profit margin goals. Yet, his peers on the company's executive committee never looked forward to his participation in the executive committee meetings. Dave was a man of strong opinions, and, unfortunately, he never hesitated to express those opinions in the strongest of manners, usually after standing up and raising his voice many decibels over the general level of conversation.

"Well, that's about the dumbest idea I've ever heard!"

"You couldn't make a good business decision if your life depended on it!"

"If I wanted your opinion, I'd.... Cancel that—I'd never want your opinion!"

It was becoming intolerable. The CEO asked the senior vice president of HR to find him a coach—otherwise, he wasn't going to last long, no matter how good his numbers were.

A coach was found and started working with him. The coach made him aware of how his actions and words affected his peers on the executive committee and coached him on other ways to channel his reactions. They did a lot of role playing, and the coach thought that they were making progress. After three sessions, Dave fired the coach, saying that he had learned all he needed to learn. The coach wasn't so sure.

Because of scheduling problems, the next executive committee meeting had been postponed until the coach had spent the three sessions with Dave. Everyone hoped that this was going to work.

About 30 minutes into the next meeting, someone said something that everyone knew would set off Dave's trigger. Dave jumped out of his seat, knocking over his chair, and glared at the person who had made the comment. He opened his mouth ... and then closed it again, picked up his chair, and sat down, never saying a word.

Obviously, the coaching was starting to take hold. Unfortunately, Dave hadn't needed to say a word—his actions said it all. He obviously still had more work to do with the coach.

━━━━━━━━

In the sidebar, the coach was successful in getting Dave to recognize the problems with his behavior and had started making some progress to change that behavior, but there was still work to do with Dave to complete the behavioral transformation. Unfortunately, Dave hadn't recognized this and ended the coaching relationship after three sessions.

Find Coaches

Coaching can come from many different sources, such as

- your manager
- a peer
- an employee
- a member of the company's HR or training staff
- a subject matter expert from another part of the company
- a faculty member from the LDP
- a member of your professional society
- an external coach.

In selecting a coach for an individual, keep in mind these basic requirements:

- The coach must have opportunities to observe the client in action. Just as you can learn a lot about your presentation skills by watching a video of yourself giving a presentation, so the coach must have opportunities to observe the client's skills that are the subject of the coaching assignment. According to Don Blohowiak, when you have to rely on the client to tell you about the problem, the coach gets "your story according to you" and that is never a complete picture. By observing the client in action, the coach gathers important data that the client doesn't have.
- The coach should have the knowledge or skills that the client needs to acquire. For example, if you want to help someone improve his or her presentation skills, the coach should have

expertise in this area. While many people can point out flaws in someone's presentation skills, you need a coach who can do more than just criticize the client's skills. The coach must be able to help the client develop the required new skills.

- There must be mutual respect between the coach and the client. Without establishing a climate of mutual respect and trust, the client will not listen to difficult messages from the coach and may not feel able to reveal confidential information that may be vital to diagnosing and correcting a problem.

- The coach should have some training and experience with coaching. While a lot of effective coaching is done informally by people without such training or experience, if you plan to introduce coaching as a learning method for LDP participants, the participants will generally feel much more comfortable with the program if they know that you have set standards for the coaches you use. This can be done by providing internal training for coaches or by looking for external coaches who have attained certification as a coach from one of the many programs accredited by the International Coach Federation (www.coachfederation.org).

Decisions on whether to use a coach versus some other learning method should be part of the process of writing each LDP participant's IDP and should involve a discussion of learning methods among the participant, the participant's manager, and the assigned HR professional. If coaching is recommended as the learning approach, the manager may sometimes volunteer to coach the participant or may have ideas about other internal or external resources who can coach the participant on the particular learning need. In other cases, the participant may have someone in mind, while in others the HR person may have to do some research to find an appropriate coach.

Tell, Teach, or Ask

Most of this section on coaching has dealt with coaching as a tool to improve participants' knowledge and skills. But there is an equally important role that coaching can play in helping participants open their minds to new

Figure 6-1. Tell–Teach–Ask model.

When employees come to you with problems, you can do any one of the following:

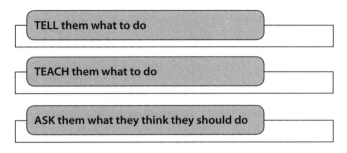

ideas and learn to trust their own ideas. One proven model is called "Tell-Teach-Ask," as shown in figure 6-1.

When employees come to their managers with problems, the managers have three choices of how to respond. The manager can do any one of the following:

- *TELL the employee what to do.* This gets the problem solved quickly with the manager's preferred solution. The difficulty is that the employee has not learned anything—if a similar, but not identical problem arises in the future, the employee will typically go back to the manager for a solution. Telling can be the right answer in an emergency situation, where quick action is needed, or when there is a safety or legal issue involved and the manager has to ensure that the employee does exactly what the manager wants done. But there is little or no learning that takes place on the part of the employee with this solution.

- *TEACH the employee what to do.* "Here's how I think about a problem like this," the manager might say, and then lead the employee through the problem-solving process. This takes more time than simply telling the employee what to do to resolve the problem, but it will result in the employee's being able to solve similar problems in the future without asking for the manager's input. Of course, this process also limits the employee to solving the problem in the same way the manager would, which can be positive but also can limit the employee from coming up with a better solution.

- *ASK how the employee thinks the problem should be solved.* This can be the right approach in several circumstances. First, if the manager doesn't know or isn't certain how to resolve the problem, this approach can yield a better resolution. Second, in some cases, the manager believes that the employee is able to solve the problem but doesn't have the confidence to apply a solution, which can reinforce the manager's faith in the employee's judgment. Third, even if the manager can solve the problem quickly, this type of conversation can yield a better solution (two heads are better than one).

A very effective senior executive once commented that whenever he put together a problem-solving task force, he always included a "smart dummy" in the group. A smart dummy, he explained, was a very bright individual who had no relevant knowledge of the situation and could ask the dumb questions that got other task force members to question their assumptions about the problem and consider alternative approaches to its resolution.

Coaches can play this role by asking questions of their clients that get them to question their own assumptions, to verbalize ideas they have kept hidden away, and to help the client act on the best of those ideas. In this type of coaching situation, it is not necessary for the coach to have subject matter expertise, but requires that the coach ask the right questions and to challenge the client's thinking processes.

Reinforcing Learning

As discussed in chapter 3, there are a number of ways to reinforce learning from LDP education sessions. Reinforcement of learning on the job helps the participants transform the information they received in the LDP education session into their personal knowledge by applying it to their work. Action-learning projects are the primary method used to provide such reinforcement, but you can also try to actively involve the LDP participants' managers in reinforcing the application of their learning to their current jobs. Remember that while the LDP is primarily designed to prepare Hi-Pos for future leadership roles in the company, there can also be great benefit from their application of much of their learning to their current jobs, and no one can reinforce the application of their learning to their current work better than their managers.

You will also find that as the LDP participants get to know each other, work together, and build trust with each other, they will reinforce each other's learning. This reinforcement behavior will grow even more valuable as the participants grow into leadership positions in the company and use the relationships they built through the LDP to get work accomplished.

Summary

Mentoring, coaching, and learning reinforcement is the fourth and final building block of the LDP model presented in this book. Both mentoring and coaching are valuable tools that belong in your leadership development tool kit to help develop your company's next generation of leaders. Reinforcement of learning back on the job helps LDP participants transform the information they received in the education sessions into their personal knowledge.

We'll now move on to assessment and evaluation in chapter 7.

Chapter 7

Participant Assessment and Program Evaluation

What's In This Chapter

- How can you use assessments (beyond the 360-degree) in the LDP?
- How can you assess the progress made by LDP participants?
- How can you assess the overall success of your LDP?

This chapter will start by examining the use of assessments, beyond the 360-degree assessment covered in chapter 5, within the leadership development program to help participants learn more about themselves and their leadership styles and to help guide their development into the next generation of company leaders. It is also important to track the progress of participants within and without the LDP to help provide valuable information to company leaders on which participants are making the most progress, which should be considered in succession plans, and which should possibly be dropped from the program. Finally, the chapter will look at how to evaluate the LDP as a whole—has all of the work that has gone into the program met the program's goals?

Using Assessments in the LDP Education Sessions

As discussed in chapter 5, the use of a 360-degree assessment for each LDP participant is a fundamental building block of the entire program. But what about the use of other assessment instruments within the program? There is certainly no lack of assessment instruments on the market. Along with well-known and widely used assessments, such as the Myers-Briggs Type Indicator and DiSC, there are hundreds of other instruments available, and each company and consultant selling those instruments will tell you that theirs is the key to self-understanding and improved performance.

It is beyond the scope of this book to recommend any particular assessment instrument. Rather, here are some guidelines for selecting and using assessments:

- The use of an assessment must be part of the plan for a specific LDP education session. As you select presenters for the education sessions, they will probably have their own favorite instruments that they have been working with and teaching for some time. The assessment should fit in with the topic of the education session and be an integral part of the participants' education in the session. Too many times have presenters used an instrument only because it provides variety in the session and gives the presenter a break while the participants complete the assessment.
- Make certain that the instruments have been tested for statistical reliability and validity. Just as with the criteria for selecting a 360-degree assessment vendor, the vendor will have psychometricians on staff or will be able to provide a report from an independent psychometrician on this. One thing to watch out for here is that some consultants that you may consider as session faculty have created their own instruments, based on their particular approach to the subject matter, but have not taken the time to validate the instruments.
- Look for instruments that come with solid educational materials to help the participants understand the results. Again, too many

instruments give you a scoring sheet and perhaps one chart showing how various categories of results relate to each other— "take the instrument, see your results, and move on to the next topic" is not a proper way to use any assessment instrument. You want to ensure that there is real learning that comes from the use of any assessment, to help participants learn about themselves, learn about differences between themselves and others, and learn how to effectively deal with those differences.

- Some assessment companies require that a person using the instrument be trained and certified on that instrument. Note that for some of the most popular assessments on the market, competitors have created clones of the original instrument that will yield the same scoring, but do not require that the person using the instrument be certified. This is not a good practice. If your presenters have the required certification, that is a good sign. But also ask the presenters how much experience they have with the instrument, review the presenters' instructional materials connected with use of the instrument, and get references from other clients of the presenters.

- Some assessment vendors require that the presenter make clear that the results of their assessment are confidential, that is, that the person taking the assessment does not have to share results with the presenter, fellow participants, or anyone else. You must honor this, but you can ask participants at the beginning of the LDP for a blanket permission to share the results with other participants within the class for discussion purposes, and with their managers and the assigned HR staff members so that the results can be considered in writing IDPs.

- Any assessment you use must be designed to help the participants better understand themselves, others, and how to work with others. The results of any assessment should never be used to put a label on someone. There have been too many instances where companies not only have used an assessment to put a label on each person, but also have made each person wear a badge or put a large notice in the office announcing that label.

- Remember that the results from any assessment are only as good as the input from the individual being assessed. If the participants answer the assessment questions honestly, the assessment will yield useful information. If the participants answer the questions in the way they think the questions should be answered, or try to manipulate the answers to put themselves in the best light, the results will be skewed.

Self-Delusion

I once used a well-known instrument on how people deal with conflict with my company's executive staff—the CEO and his direct reports. When we shared results from the instrument, one vice president reported his result as being very accommodating, that is, that he would bend over backward to make certain that other people's concerns were addressed before his own. When he reported his result, the rest of the group burst out in laughter—they saw him as the most competitive, win-at-all-costs, and take-no-prisoners person they had ever worked with.

Obviously, either this vice president saw himself differently than how others saw him or he answered the questions the way he thought they should be answered, rather than completing the instrument honestly.

The good result here is that this led to a frank discussion of the vice president's style and both better self-understanding on his part and better understanding of him by the other executive staff members.

There are many good assessment instruments on the market, as well as a lot of junk. Selecting assessment instruments and using them as an integral part of the LDP education sessions can add richness to the program and provide participants with important insights into themselves and others with whom they work.

Evaluating Participants

The purpose of the LDP is to ensure that your company has the talent it needs to lead the company in the future. The LDP itself is a great vehicle for developing your Hi-Pos, but not everyone who is selected to participate will perform at equally high levels. That is why the LDP is also an effective way to cull the wheat from the chaff, to see who is ready to lead and who is not before you make costly errors in selecting successors for your current leadership team.

Throughout the LDP, you and your company's executives will have many opportunities to view the performance of the participants. Rather than have each participant evaluated solely on the basis of infrequent observations, create individual participant performance records that include the following:

- *Notes on individual performance within each education session.* Was the individual an active participant or a sideline observer? How well did the individual perform on any in-class tasks? Did the individual take the initiative in brainstorming and other interactive learning activities, or did the individual let other people do the work? Have several observers (the LDP manager and some HR staff) in each education session make notes on individual performance. You can also ask the presenter for any observations made of the individual participants.
- *Notes on individual performance on action-learning projects.* Did the individual do a fair share of the work? How well did the individual work with other members of the team (for team-based action-learning projects)? Did the individual step up to lead the team or just let other people take on that responsibility? How good were the results of each action-learning project? Did the individual follow through on the project to find ways of applying the project to a larger audience? If the action-learning project was not successful, or reported suboptimal results, what did the individual learn from the project (as reflected in the project debrief as explained in chapter 4)? Did the individual take what was learned in the action-learning project and apply it to daily work to improve on-the-job performance? On team-based action-learning projects, you may want to have the team members rate each other (see exhibit 7-1). These rating sheets should be collected and tallied by the LDP manager or by the HR staff who acted as team coaches on the action-learning projects and

should become part of each participant's LDP performance record. If you are using HR staff as team coaches on these projects, they can also add their own comments based on their observations of the team.

- *Personal vision statement.* If, as recommended, you have the LDP participants write a personal vision statement as the action-learning assignment following the first LDP education session, include that statement in the participant's record.

- *Observations of the executive review panels for the action-learning projects.* How good was the project? How well did the participant perform in presenting the project to the panel? How well did the participant respond to questions from the panel? If the project was unsuccessful, or achieved suboptimal results, what did the participant learn from the experience? These notes and observations can be collected from the panel members by the LDP manager and included in each participant's record.

- *Observations from each participant's manager.* Was the participant able to handle his or her regular job along with the demands of the LDP? Was the participant able to use what he or she learned in the LDP to improve performance in the individual's regular jobs?

- *Notes on the 360-degree assessment and on each participant's IDP.* How well did the participant respond to the feedback from the 360-degree assessment? How active a role did the participant play in writing the IDP? Was the individual serious about the IDP, or did the participant complete it just to check it off from the list of requirements? Did the participant follow through on the developmental activities listed in the IDP/learning contract?

- *Observations from the coach.* If the participant was assigned a coach to help improve some aspect of performance, the coach can also provide input to the LDP performance record. How seriously did the participant take the coaching? How active a role did the participant take in the coaching sessions? How quickly did the coaching result in behavioral changes? Did the participant's job performance improve as a result of the coaching?

- *Observations from mentor.* Similarly, each participant's mentor can provide input to the LDP performance record. What impressed

Exhibit 7-1. Team member rating sheet.

Name: _____

Names of other team members: _____
_____
_____

Who acted as team leader for this project? _____

Action-learning project title: _____

Please complete the following ratings for yourself and for each of your fellow team members. Circle the appropriate rating.

Name of Team Member	Low						High
A. Level of cooperation with other team members	1	2	3	4	5	6	7
B. Initiative taken	1	2	3	4	5	6	7
C. Thoroughness of work	1	2	3	4	5	6	7
D. Timeliness of work	1	2	3	4	5	6	7
E. Quality of work	1	2	3	4	5	6	7
F. Willingness to help other team members	1	2	3	4	5	6	7
G. Effectiveness as a team member	1	2	3	4	5	6	7

Comments: _____

Name of Team Member	Low						High
A. Level of cooperation with other team members	1	2	3	4	5	6	7
B. Initiative taken	1	2	3	4	5	6	7
C. Thoroughness of work	1	2	3	4	5	6	7
D. Timeliness of work	1	2	3	4	5	6	7
E. Quality of work	1	2	3	4	5	6	7
F. Willingness to help other team members	1	2	3	4	5	6	7
G. Effectiveness as a team member	1	2	3	4	5	6	7

Comments: _____

(continued on next page)

Exhibit 7-1. Team member rating sheet (continued).

Name of Team Member	Low						High
A. Level of cooperation with other team members	1	2	3	4	5	6	7
B. Initiative taken	1	2	3	4	5	6	7
C. Thoroughness of work	1	2	3	4	5	6	7
D. Timeliness of work	1	2	3	4	5	6	7
E. Quality of work	1	2	3	4	5	6	7
F. Willingness to help other team members	1	2	3	4	5	6	7
G. Effectiveness as a team member	1	2	3	4	5	6	7

Comments: _____

Name of Team Member	Low						High
A. Level of cooperation with other team members	1	2	3	4	5	6	7
B. Initiative taken	1	2	3	4	5	6	7
C. Thoroughness of work	1	2	3	4	5	6	7
D. Timeliness of work	1	2	3	4	5	6	7
E. Quality of work	1	2	3	4	5	6	7
F. Willingness to help other team members	1	2	3	4	5	6	7
G. Effectiveness as a team member	1	2	3	4	5	6	7

Comments: _____

the mentor most about the participant? What weaknesses did the mentor notice in the participant? How good a fit does the participant have with the company's culture and values?

Make all of this data and the observations part of each participant's LDP performance record. Ultimately, it will need to be compiled by the assigned HR staff member for presentation by the senior executive within the participant's business unit or function to an executive talent review session.

Executive Talent Reviews

In the book, *Execution: The Discipline of Getting Things Done,* Larry Bossidy, then CEO of Allied Signal, stated his belief that the development of employees is a major responsibility of a company's CEO, and that he personally spent up to 30 percent of his time on development issues (Bossidy et al., 2002).

While Bossidy's focus on employee development is unusual, you and your CEO need to understand that conducting executive talent reviews takes a major commitment of time from the company's executives. Most CEOs, when challenged, will admit that despite their many other priorities and challenges, ensuring the development of leadership talent for the near-term and long-term future must be one of their top priorities.

You already conducted one executive talent review to select the pool of Hi-Pos to be included in the LDP. Now that you have concluded the first complete cycle of the LDP, you have a lot more data on each person in that pool, meaning that the executive talent review you conduct now should be much richer. How do you prepare for it? What roles do the company's HR staff, the executives, the LDP manager, and others play in the review?

Human Resources' Role

Throughout this process, you will have accumulated a huge amount of information about each high-potential employee that you included in the LDP. It is the role of the HR staff to collect all of this information and prepare a summary report for the executive talent review meetings.

From the original process of identifying Hi-Pos, you gathered information on each LDP participant with regard to your company's key competencies, leading indicators for the company's future leaders, performance reviews, and other data.

Now, you also have for each participant the following additional information:

- Start with the results of the 360-degree review done early in the LDP. If you chose to do a second 360-degree review at the end of the program, this would give you some measure of progress on key competencies. You may also have done other assessments in conjunction with LDP education sessions, as discussed earlier in this chapter, and these may yield some useful data as well.

- Each participant created a personal leadership vision statement as the action-learning assignment after the first LDP education session. If you chose to do so, each participant would have revised their vision statements for the last LDP education session.

- You will have the results of a number of action-learning projects that each participant completed. Along with the actual results, you will have the information provided in the project debriefings, which can provide clues to how much each participant learned from those projects. For those projects that were done by teams of participants, rather than by individual participants, you also have team ratings done by fellow team members.

- From each participant's IDP, you have information on learning goals outside of the formal LDP education sessions and a learning contract for each participant. The learning contract should be updated by the participant, the participant's manager, and the assigned HR staff member to provide the latest information on how well the contract was fulfilled.

- Depending on the length of your LDP, you will have one or two additional performance reviews done by each participant's manager. These can provide good information on whether the participant was able to apply the learning from the LDP to make a positive difference in on-the-job performance.

- Faculty (internal or external) used in the LDP education sessions may have some relevant insights on some participants, and those should be included with the other data.

- If you instituted a mentoring program, you will have input from each participant's mentor on progress made.

- If you assigned a coach to a participant as part of the IDP, you can get input from the coach on progress made.
- At various times during the program, the company's executives had opportunities to work with the LDP group, as speakers, as session faculty, and as members of the project review panels. These executives' observations should be included with the other data.

It is the job of the HR staff to collect all of this data, process it into findings and recommendations on each participant's performance and potential, and then share it with the appropriate executive so that the executive can take the lead in the discussion of each participant who falls into a particular area of control, for example, the vice president of marketing would lead the discussion on any LDP participants who come from the marketing function.

Executive's Role

First, each executive who takes part in the executive talent reviews must make a commitment of time to do them well. The discussion of each LDP participant will take from 30 to 60 minutes. Thus, if you have 20 to 50 participants in the program, the talent review sessions can take anywhere from 10 to 50 hours to complete—that's one very long day to more than a week of dedicated time just for the LDP participants (and there are likely other talent reviews that can be conducted on employees who were not in the LDP).

Second, while the HR staff will have compiled all of the data on each LDP participant, as described above, it is up to the executives in charge of each business unit and functional area to become fully familiar with the data for each person within their realm. Based on all of the data, and on discussions with their own staff and the assigned HR staff prior to the talent review meeting, the executives should take responsibility to make the initial presentation of each candidate to the talent review meeting and to make recommendations for the next steps for each candidate they present. This can take a half day to a full day of the executive's time to prepare for each candidate.

In addition to presenting and discussing each candidate from their own area of responsibility, executives may have input to the discussion of other candidates based on the following:

- observations of participants in their roles as faculty, dinner speakers, and action-learning project review panel members
- interactions with any participants for whom they acted as mentors
- interactions or observations of participants made as part of other company business.

The talent review meetings are prime opportunities for executives to learn about the company's talent who may not have been directly in their chain of command or line of sight and to offer developmental opportunities for that talent (for example, an executive may suggest that a talented engineering manager could develop a better sense of the business by taking an assignment in the marketing group).

The executives on the talent review panel will take these responsibilities only as seriously as the CEO does. If the CEO doesn't believe in this process, other executives are less likely to devote the required time to do it right.

LDP Manager's Role

The LDP manager has played a unique role in the entire LDP process. The manager is probably the only person who has been to every LDP session; attended all virtual follow-up sessions; read every IDP, personal leadership vision statement, and action-learning report; and had frequent contact with all of the LDP participants throughout the entire program. While the LDP manager has provided some of the data collected by the HR staff to prepare for the executive talent reviews, the LDP manager can also participate in the talent review sessions to provide any insights that he or she may have developed over the course of the program.

Other Roles

In addition to the executives, HR staff, and LDP manager, there are several other people who may participate in the talent review sessions, albeit only while specific LDP participants are being discussed:

- the LDP participant's manager
- the LDP participant's mentor (if you have instituted a mentoring program)
- the LDP participant's coach (if you have instituted a coaching program).

Decisions

At this point, LDP participants have had at least one previous talent review, that is, the one where they were designated as having high potential and then placed into the LDP. With the completion of the LDP (covering one to two years) and the wealth of information about each participant coming from the program, a different set of decisions needs to be made:

- Some participants may be ready for immediate promotion, so the executive review team may want to discuss what opportunities there are currently and in the short-term future for them. It is also very possible that there are participants who are ready for promotion but for whom there are no open slots. These participants should be placed in a promotion pool and informed that they will be considered for promotion as openings arise. To keep them engaged while they wait, the executive review committee may decide to give them some interim assignments, such as to head up a cross-functional task force.
- Some participants may be judged to be very good in their current roles, but lack the qualities and track record (as demonstrated from the collected information) to be considered for promotion. These people should be kept in their current roles, and it should be explained to them why they are not being considered for promotion in the near term.
- Some participants may be judged to need additional experience before they are ready to assume a leadership position in the company. In these cases, the executive review team will want to discuss how to provide the additional experience, for example, by some short-term assignments in other business units or by taking an overseas assignment for a period of time.

- Some (hopefully very few) participants may be judged to have failed the LDP. That is, they may not have performed well in education sessions or action-learning projects and weren't able to transfer what they learned in the LDP to make any noticeable difference in their job performance. The executive review committee may then need to make some difficult decisions as to whether to terminate these employees.

Schedule the executive talent review of LDP graduates as soon as possible after the completion of the program, because the participants will naturally be anxious to learn what opportunities await them as a result of all their hard work during the program. If you wait too long to conduct the talent review and to start announcing its results, you may find that some of the participants will start peddling their new knowledge and skills to other employers.

Evaluating the Overall Value of Your LDP

Too many training organizations rely on end-of-course participant evaluations to judge the quality and value of their programs. While these smile sheets can provide valuable information on the topics and faculty you selected for LDP education sessions, they are not sufficient to prove the worth of the program to the participants or to the company executives who are footing the bill for the program.

Chapter 2 described a set of reasonable expectations for the LDP. These are repeated below with further explanation. The basic evaluation method for the LDP is to measure whether these expectations have been met.

Expectation 1: Through a comprehensive set of educational sessions focused on your company's key competencies, you will help participants develop the business acumen and execution skills they will need when they assume new leadership roles.

If, as explained in chapter 2, you planned your LDP education agenda with input from company executives and participants, you will have met this expectation. Another factor that might affect this expectation is the length of your LDP—if you planned the program to have only four education sessions over a one-year period versus eight or nine sessions over a two-year period, you just won't be able to cover as many topics.

Expectation 2: You will expand and improve the quality of your company's bench strength and have a larger pool of qualified talent when developing the company's succession plans.

While this should be self-evident after the post-program executive review, the executive panel should pass judgment on whether or not this is true.

Expectation 3: You will retain some of your top talent you might not otherwise have kept—employees who see that the company is investing in their future with the company are more likely to stay. For many employees who were not selected for the LDP, you will create an incentive to improve their performance so that they can qualify for the next group of LDP participants.

This measurement should be self-evident. How many people started in your LDP, and how many were still with the company at its conclusion? How does this compare with the retention rates elsewhere in the company? As the LDP progressed, how many non-LDP employees asked their managers, HR, or the LDP program manager how they could get into the next LDP group?

Expectation 4: Through action-learning projects, you will solve some long-standing company challenges that might otherwise never have been addressed.

Again, whether this expectation is met should be self-evident. Did executives identify some long-standing challenges to be assigned as action-learning projects? If they did, were the action-learning projects successful in meeting those challenges? Remember that not all action-learning projects will reach a successful conclusion, and that significant learning can still take place for participants who failed to achieve the goals of their projects.

Expectation 5: You will make visible to the company's executive team a wide range of talent that they might otherwise never have seen.

Only the executives who participated in the LDP in some way (as faculty, guest speakers, or members of an action-learning project review panel) can determine whether this expectation was met. Most executives' line of sight within a company is limited to their direct reports, their peers, and those higher in the organization. Most executives who have participated in an LDP say the following:

- Their views of the organization have broadened.
- They feel more connected to the front lines of the business.
- They have identified one or more people in other parts of the business they would like to recruit into their organizations.
- They are impressed and heartened by the talent they have seen from across the company.

Expectation 6: You will see participants improve their performance in their current jobs as a result of what they learn in the LDP.

The best judges of this expectation are the participants' direct managers. Evidence of this will come from comparing participants' performance reviews before, during, and at the conclusion of the LDP.

Expectation 7: You will be able to weed out some employees who had seemed to be rising stars, but who failed to perform well in the LDP. This will help the company avoid potentially costly promotional errors.

People don't generally like to see others fail, especially when you hand select them to be part of a program you have designed. But if you have even one person who had been seen as a rising star in the company but who fails to meet expectations, the savings to the company from avoiding just that one promotional error may be greater than the entire cost of the LDP. The ability to test the leadership capabilities of LDP participants through the action-learning projects can be the most valuable aspect of the program to executives who have to make promotion and succession decisions.

Expectation 8: You will help company executives feel more connected to many parts of the business through their participation in the LDP.

Most executives who have participated in an LDP report that this has oc-curred and that they got a lot more from the experience than they gave.

Of course, the final question for the executives that will be the ultimate evaluation measure for the LDP is, "Now that the first LDP class has graduated and you have reviewed the results for this group, *do you want to run the program again* for another group of Hi-Pos?"

Summary

Throughout the LDP, you collected large amounts of information about the participants—through observing them in the classroom and on their action-learning projects, from the 360-degree assessments and any other assessment instruments you chose to include in the program, and from their coaches and mentors. All of this data is valuable and should become part of the executive talent review conducted at the conclusion of the LDP.

To evaluate the overall value of the LDP, go back to the expectations that were set for the program before it began. Have you been able to meet those expectations? Ultimately, the company's current leadership will provide the final verdict on the program's success: Do they want to run the LDP again for another group of Hi-Pos?

The book has shown the many people who must contribute to the plan-ning and execution of your company's LDP. Chapter 8 will provide a summary of these roles and responsibilities.

Chapter 8

Roles in the LDP

═══════════

What's In This Chapter

- Who needs to be involved in the planning and execution of your LDP, and what roles do they need to play?
- What is the role of the LDP manager?

═══════════

Building a successful leadership development program for your company involves many organizational players with specific roles and responsibilities that contribute to its success. You will likely involve the following people or departments:

- HR department
- LDP manager
- training department
- executive staff
- line management
- IT department
- marketing department.

Additionally, you will need to call on external resources including the following:

- people who will serve as faculty for the education sessions
- hotel or conference center staff.

This chapter will review the roles that each of these people or groups needs to play to make your LDP optimally successful.

Human Resources Department Roles

In larger companies, leadership development may be its own department with a staff dedicated to identifying and developing Hi-Pos at many different levels. Unfortunately, most small to mid-sized companies do not have the luxury of having dedicated staff for this purpose. In these smaller companies, the LDP will typically be started and run by the HR staff. Their involvement starts with the identification of the Hi-Pos who will participate in the LDP, as explained in chapter 1. HR's responsibilities include the following:

- working with company executives to gain their participation in the LDP and coaching them on their roles in the LDP
- gathering of information for the initial talent reviews where participants are nominated to the program (chapter 1)
- assigning HR staff to act as observers in the LDP education sessions (chapter 3)
- working with company executives to identify topics for the LDP education sessions and action-learning projects (chapters 3 and 4)
- assigning team coaches for action-learning teams (chapter 4)
- administering the 360-degree assessments (chapter 5)
- working with participants and their managers to write IDPs (chapter 5)
- assigning mentors to LDP participants, training mentors and mentoring clients (LDP participants), and briefing the participants' managers on the mentoring program (chapter 6)

- identifying internal or external coaches to help participants fulfill their IDPs and learning contracts (chapter 6)
- summarizing all data gathered on participants throughout the program and briefing executives prior to the post-program executive talent review (chapter 7)
- appointing an LDP manager, as discussed below.

LDP Manager Role

Before the LDP can begin, HR should appoint a manager for the LDP who will coordinate and manage all aspects of the program. The LDP manager should report to the head of HR. The primary responsibilities of the LDP manager are as follows:

- Plan each session, including selection of faculty (chapter 3).
- Arrange for follow-up to education sessions (chapter 3).
- Assign action-learning projects to teams or individuals for each education session (chapter 4).
- Recruit executives to serve on the action-learning project review panels (chapter 4).
- Arrange for other executive participation in the LDP, such as dinner speakers at the education sessions (chapter 3).
- Work with the assigned meeting planner with regard to selecting sites for LDP education sessions and all logistical arrangements (chapter 10).
- Plan and manage the budget for the LDP (chapter 10).
- Serve as the moderator for all LDP sessions to provide a single point of contact for participants and to ensure continuity across all program activities (chapter 3).
- Be an observer of participation in all LDP activities (chapter 7).

The LDP manager is an important full-time role. Typically, it should be someone from the HR staff or from the training group who is familiar with the company and has a good background in management and leadership development and has the trust of the head of HR and the executive staff.

Training Department Roles

The roles of your company's training staff will depend on the scope of the training organization. Each of the roles listed below can be filled by your company's training staff if they have the capabilities to do so. Otherwise, you will have to outsource those functions that don't exist in-house. The following are possible roles for the training staff with respect to the LDP:

- The LDP manager can come from the company's training organization if it has a person with the right capabilities, as outlined above.
- An in-house instructional designer can be assigned to work with any executives who will act as faculty to help them prepare materials for and structure their presentations.
- Training staff can often use their own networks to identify external faculty to teach various LDP education sessions.
- Training staff can help brainstorm ideas for action-learning projects for each of the LDP education sessions.
- Training staff who have appropriate backgrounds and experience can teach some LDP education sessions (chapter 3).
- If your company has its own training facilities, the training staff can take responsibility for meeting logistics for all LDP education sessions that will take place in those facilities (chapter 9).

Executive Staff Roles

As described throughout the book, company executives have many roles to play in the LDP:

- selecting LDP participants through the process of identifying Hi-Pos (chapter 1)
- acting as dinner speakers who then conduct open question-and-answer sessions with LDP participants (one per LDP education session; chapters 2 and 3)
- serving as faculty or co-presenters in LDP education sessions (chapter 3)

- identifying and prioritizing topics for LDP education sessions (chapter 3)
- identifying and prioritizing action-learning projects (chapter 4)
- acting as mentors to LDP participants (chapter 6)
- conducting post-program executive talent reviews to evaluate individual participants and the overall program (chapters 1 and 7).

It is especially important that the company's CEO take an active role in the first LDP education session as a dinner speaker. It is also very helpful if the CEO can arrange to attend dinners at other LDP education sessions occasionally. The CEO's continued participation in the LDP stresses the importance of the program and the participants' work in the program more than anything else.

Line Management Roles

While the roles listed below are focused primarily on those line managers whose direct reports are participating in the LDP, it is important that you make all managers in the company aware of the LDP and ask for their cooperation in its execution. This starts with the identification of Hi-Pos (chapter 1). Even if a manager does not have a direct report in the LDP, the manager may be asked to act as a coach or to cooperate with LDP participants in their action-learning projects.

For those managers who have direct reports participating in the LDP, you should ask their cooperation in the following:

- enabling participants to take the time to attend LDP education sessions and to work on their action-learning projects (without the managers' cooperation, the participants will have a much more difficult time in fulfilling the requirements of the LDP)
- cooperating with the HR staff and the LDP manager to collect information on employee performance for individual and program evaluation purposes
- working with participants and the assigned HR staff in completing the 360-degree assessments for those participants and then

working with the participants and the assigned HR staff to write each participant's IDP (chapter 5)

- coaching LDP participants as they apply what they have learned in the LDP to their daily work (line managers may also be asked to coach, where appropriate, other LDP participants who may not be their direct reports; chapter 6).

Information Technology Department Roles

Enlist the cooperation of your IT group to assist the LDP operation in the following ways:

- ensuring that participants have access to their company email and voicemail accounts no matter where the LDP sessions are being held
- setting up of discussion forums for LDP participants as well as for teams of participants to use in their action-learning projects
- providing technical support if an LDP education session requires IT capabilities (e.g., if you are running a network-based simulation as part of an education session, it may be necessary to set up a network at the site of the training and provide on-site technical support to ensure that the application runs properly)
- setting up of web conferencing capabilities to conduct virtual follow-up sessions (these capabilities may also be useful for team action-learning projects to enable the teams to work together; chapter 3).

Marketing Department Roles

In many companies, the marketing group includes one or more meeting planners who can provide assistance with finding facilities for LDP education sessions and with other logistical requirements. The marketing group can also help with program literature and any awards that you may plan to give at the end of the program (chapter 9).

External Resources Roles

Chapter 3 has already discussed in detail the roles of external faculty for the LDP education sessions. These roles include the following:

- customizing content to the needs of the company and the LDP participants
- conducting virtual follow-up sessions
- recommending action-learning project topics that will use the content of the educational sessions
- participating in a discussion forum with participants to continue to answer questions after the education session.

The other external groups that you may use are the sales staffs at any hotel or conference center you choose to host your education sessions. More guidelines for working with these external resources will be discussed in chapter 10.

Summary

There are many people who need to be involved in the planning and execution of your company's LDP. U.S. Secretary of State Hilary Rodham Clinton wrote a book titled *It Takes a Village*. Similarly, it takes the efforts of the entire company to develop its next generation of leaders. This is a major reason why you need to appoint a full-time LDP manager to coordinate all of these resources and ensure that everything goes according to plan.

The next chapter will provide advice on how to get started with building your company's own LDP.

Chapter 9

Getting Started

What's In This Chapter

- How do you get your LDP started?
- What commitments should you ask LDP participants to make?
- How do you bring closure to the LDP?

To make your leadership development program successful, many steps must be taken. It starts with agreement among your company's HR group and your CEO and other executives that you want to build an LDP, consensus on a set of goals for the LDP, and approval of a budget for the program. As will be discussed in chapter 10, there are many cost alternatives, so your LDP can be as lavish or as frugal as the budget and the company's culture allow.

Once there is agreement to build the LDP, you must identify a manager for the program and hold a planning meeting. This meeting should start with a half-day to a full-day meeting (it will take more than one meeting to properly plan the LDP). In attendance at the meeting should be the LDP manager, the head of HR, the head of the company's training group (if you have one), and other HR business partners who know the business concerns of the company's various business units and functional areas.

You may also want to include in the planning meeting an influential member of the company's executive staff who can represent the executives' interests in the planning of the LDP. If your HR business partners are well informed of the executives' business agendas, this representation may not be needed, but you will still want the executives to review and approve your final plans for the LDP.

The agenda for this first LDP planning meeting will include the following:

- discussing the full LDP model and which portions of the model will be included in your company's LDP implementation
- discussing how you will identify the group of Hi-Pos who will be asked to participate in the LDP, including how to ensure that you have representation from all business units, all functional groups, and all geographic areas, as well as a target size for the group
- discussing how long the LDP should last (one to two years) and how many education sessions should be included in the program
- brainstorming a list of topics for the LDP education sessions (a list of potential topics can be found in the appendix to this book)
- brainstorming the types of action-learning projects that might be assigned to follow up on each of the education sessions
- starting the planning process for conducting 360-degree assessments and writing IDPs for LDP participants
- discussing how the mentoring program will be structured and who from the company's executive staff would make the best mentors
- discussing locations where you might hold LDP education sessions
- defining roles and responsibilities for various components of the LDP (discussed in chapter 8) and how to enlist the support of

the HR staff, training staff, IT staff, company executives, and others who will be involved in making the LDP a success

- deciding how you will evaluate each LDP participant and the LDP as a whole.

Once consensus has been reached on all of the above, assign responsibility to the LDP manager and others to create plans for the various aspects of the project.

This chapter will focus on practical advice on many of these topics, beginning with when and where to hold the LDP education sessions.

Selecting Dates and Locations

When selecting dates for the LDP education sessions, keep in mind your company's business cycles. Typically, you won't want to schedule a session for the last month of your fiscal quarter because people will be working too hard to meet that quarter's business goals. Similarly, if your sales staff is on monthly quotas, you probably don't want to schedule a session for the last week of the month. In the sample schedules shown in chapter 3, each education session starts on Sunday. While this has worked in many companies, determine whether this fits in with your company's culture and business practices. Starting on Sundays does eat into the participants' weekends, but you are asking participants to make some sacrifices and add some hours to their work schedules to participate, so this can work.

You also need to decide on the length of the overall program. It is recommended that the LDP contain eight or nine education sessions over a period of two years, although you may also opt for making it a one-year program with four or five education sessions or an 18-month program with six or seven education sessions. Shortening the program to less than a year doesn't allow participants enough time to build their relationships and networks or for executives to observe participants' performance in the LDP.

Many companies, in an effort to save money, would like to hold the education sessions at the company headquarters. Not only does it save money on renting other facilities, but it also lessens the time requirements for executives from the headquarters location to participate in the program. Before making this decision, first ask yourself if you have a good space in which to hold the program. Jamming everyone into the boardroom just to save the cost of renting meeting space elsewhere can be counterproductive. Other reasons to consider holding the program off-site include the following:

- If you hold the program at the company headquarters, many participants from out of town will be tempted to sneak away to conduct meetings with headquarters personnel whom they rarely see otherwise. This can be counterproductive to the goals of the LDP. Instead, think about finding a hotel or conference facility near company headquarters. Also, in scheduling the LDP, allow the participants an extra day or two of travel so that they can take care of headquarters business before or after the program.

- When the LDP education sessions are held off-site, it helps the participants to focus on the program content. Their focus during the program should be on learning, not on other company business. At the same time, because the participants are all top performers (or they wouldn't have been selected for the LDP), they are going to want to take care of business matters even while they are at the LDP session. So, in scheduling your sessions, allow time for them to check their email and voicemail and to make necessary phone calls, but if you can possibly do so, require that they turn off their laptops, cell phones, and PDAs during the program sessions. Establish an emergency number where people can leave messages or, in dire emergencies, call them out of the program to take care of pressing business.

- Consider whether using company facilities can create an atmosphere that is conducive to learning. If you have a state-of-the-art training center that is set apart from other company business facilities, it may be suitable.

- While you don't want to pamper the participants too much, you do want to make them comfortable. Breaking from an education session to go to a separate dining area provides a welcome break in the day, as opposed to having sandwiches brought in to an already crowded headquarters conference room. If you hold the session at a hotel or conference center, there will also be other amenities available that will make the atmosphere more conducive to learning and networking with each other.

- Does your company have multiple locations? If so, consider holding sessions at different locations near your major facilities. This enables executives from those facilities to participate, if only to attend a dinner with the participants. You might also consider including a tour of local facilities as part of the program; for example, have the local staff host a breakfast and tour at the start of one day's session.

- If your company has international operations, consider holding a session near your international headquarters locations.

- If an educational session requires a network of computers, for example to run a business simulation, make certain that the facility you select has the capability to support this, and make certain that your company's IT staff can set up the needed equipment and support it on-site during the program.

International Exposure for LDP Participants

In one program I ran, we held a summer session at a major British university near the company's European headquarters. We used the European executives as the action-learning project review panel and the European president to give the after-dinner presentation and conduct the question-and-answer session. It provided the non-European participants an opportunity to learn more about the company's European business and gave the European executives a view of talent in other parts of the organization that would not ordinarily have been visible to them.

Some additional tips on selecting facilities for your programs will be provided in chapter 10.

Getting Participants' Commitment

Whether your LDP design extends over one year or two years (or some other length), you want to get a commitment from the participants to stay through the entire program. The model will work best when all participants attend every session and complete all action-learning assignments.

When participants are chosen for the LDP, send each of them a letter explaining the commitment the company is seeking from them and include the following items:

- Congratulate them on being selected to participate in the LDP.
- Make it clear that participation in the LDP is not a promise of promotion—that promotions will be based on how well participants perform in all aspects of the program (as well as in their current jobs) and on the availability of suitable vacancies.
- Outline all aspects of the overall LDP, explain how long it will run, tell them that the company expects them to fully participate in the program while still doing their regular jobs, and this is estimated to add 10 percent to 15 percent to their workload.
- Explain that participation in the program will involve taking some personal assessments, in addition to the 360-degree assessment, and ask for their permission (by signing and returning the letter) to share their results in the education sessions and with their managers and assigned HR staff in writing their IDPs.
- Ask for a commitment to complete the entire program (by signing and returning a copy of the letter to the LDP manager). You may also ask for a commitment that they stay with the company for a period of time (typically equal to the length of the LDP) after completing the program. Check with your legal department to determine whether this is enforceable under applicable labor laws. In most cases, it will not be enforceable, but asking for the commitment will create an expectation.
- Explain the LDP attendance policy. You can set this however you want, but two basic rules are recommended: First, a participant can miss only one session, and that absence has to be the result of

a major illness, family crisis, or a long-standing commitment, for example, "I've been planning my wedding for three years and I cannot change the date." If a person misses two sessions, he or she is dropped from the LDP roster. Second, if a participant misses an LDP education session, it is that person's responsibility to contact other participants to learn what was missed and to select and complete an appropriate action-learning project.

Selecting Education Session Topics and Faculty

In chapter 3, an outline was given for the recommended agenda for the first LDP education session, namely to focus on the following:

- what it means to be a leader
- how leaders' careers get derailed
- some type of leadership assessment
- career choices and work–life balance.

Select session topics from your analysis of the needs of the business and of the participants. After the first session, alternate between hard topics, such as finance or innovation, and softer topics, such as coaching skills or various leadership skills. Of course, the longer the LDP, the more topics you can include in the overall education session agenda. This book's appendix contains a list of possible topics from which you can choose, giving a brief outline of each topic and the types of action-learning projects that might stem from each topic. Don't limit yourself to this list if you think of another topic that is more in line with your company's business goals and strategies and the particular needs of your group of participants.

Chapter 3 also includes a checklist of criteria for selecting faculty, while chapter 10 discusses many ways of finding faculty and the relative costs of various types of faculty. Do not scrimp on costs for the first session's faculty, because this first faculty member will set the tone for the entire program. This does not mean that you have to spend a small fortune on a name speaker, but only that you work to obtain a well-experienced faculty member who has worked effectively with similar audiences in the past. If the faculty member you select is indeed outstanding in this first session, you might also consider bringing the person back to do the last session of the LDP to provide some continuity and closure to the program.

Another common question that arises is whether you can exempt some participants from an education session whose topic they have already mastered. For example, an LDP participant from your company's finance department may ask to be exempted from an education session on finance for nonfinancial managers, or a participant from your HR staff who is certified in the Myers-Briggs Type Indicator may request exemption from a session built around the MBTI. Give no such exemptions, but instead find a way to use these participants' knowledge and skills to help other participants during the sessions. As discussed earlier, teaching is another way of demonstrating leadership. Also, allowing some participants to skip sessions hinders the development of networking and teamwork on subsequent action-learning projects.

Working With Company Executives

As discussed in earlier chapters, there are several roles that you should ask your company's executives to play in the LDP:

- education session faculty (or co-presenters)
- speakers at LDP education sessions
- dinner guests at LDP education sessions
- action-learning project review panel members.

Unless one of your company's executives is well experienced at leading education sessions on a given topic, do not use an executive as faculty in the first LDP education session. At the same time, it is very important to get your CEO involved in the first session, either to welcome participants at the opening dinner or to speak at the dinner on a later night in the first education session. The CEO's participation in the first LDP session stresses to the participants that the company is supporting the program and that their participation in the program is visible at the highest levels of the company.

Whether your CEO or another executive is selected as the first session dinner speaker, executives should spend 15 to 20 minutes speaking about their own leadership journeys, what makes the company's history and culture unique, and their brief vision of the future of the company. Following these few formal remarks, ask the executive to open the floor to any and all questions and to spend as much time as needed to answer *all* questions. There may be some inappropriate questions asked, but the audience will quickly self-regulate. Also, there may be times when the CEO or other executive will have to respond to a question with a statement like this: "Your question is a good one. But because of pending litigation (or nondisclosure agreements relating to ongoing negotiations), I cannot answer the question at this time. But I do promise you that when I can answer the question without these restraints, I will come back to this group and do so."

After the first education session, participants will begin each session by reporting on their action-learning projects to a panel of company executives. The LDP manager can recruit executive review panel members for this purpose. The panel should contain a cross-section of company executives from different business units and functional areas. If an education session is being held away from the company headquarters, the panel members should be from the geographic area in which the session is being held. If the action-learning projects for a particular session were selected by executives, try to get those executives onto the review panel.

In recruiting the members of the executive review panels beforehand, stress the following points:

- Participants were to spend four to six hours per week on the assigned action-learning projects so the results may be limited by the time allotted to the project.
- Even if the project did not achieve its stated objectives, the executives should probe what the participants learned from even a failed project.
- The review panel should ask the participants not just what they learned from the project, but also how they will apply their learning to their current jobs.

Remind executives that a benefit of participating as a review panel member is the opportunity to see a group of Hi-Pos who might not otherwise be in their line of vision.

Some companies have included members of their boards of directors in the review panels. This decision should be left up to your CEO and might be most appropriate for the final session of the LDP.

Completing Your Leadership Development Program

Whether your LDP is one year or two years long, plan a final session to bring closure to the program and to the participants. Chapter 3 recommended that for a two-year program the final action-learning project should be for the participants to update the personal vision statements that they created after the first session. This gives participants an opportunity to present their revised vision statements along with statements of what they had learned over the two years and how it has affected them and their careers.

This is the ideal time to have the review panel include the CEO, other executives, and perhaps members of your company's board of directors. In previous sessions, the time allocation for presentation of action-learning project results was limited to the first afternoon. For these final presentations, allow sufficient time for all LDP participants to make their presentations to the full audience, even if this takes a full day. The review panel should take careful notes from these presentations, because what they hear from the participants should certainly be brought into the executive talent reviews that will follow the completion of the program.

Assuming that the LDP has gone well, make the final session a celebration of the program, the participants, and the participants' achievements over the course of the program. If your company can afford it, and if it fits into the company's culture, you might consider presenting certificates or plaques to each participant at the close of the final session. And, given the investments of time and other sacrifices that participants and their families have made to be part of the program, you might consider including the participants' spouses or significant others in a gala final dinner.

This may also be the right time to use the same faculty as you did in the first LDP session to bring closure to the program. If possible, it could also be the right time to announce some promotions of LDP participants that resulted from their performance in the program.

At the end of this final session, evaluation of the overall LDP should be done in writing by the participants and by the executives who have been involved in the program, as discussed in chapter 7. Plan to conduct an executive talent review as quickly after the completion of the program as possible, allowing time for the LDP manager and the HR staff to complete preparation of all of the materials for each participant. There are, of course, several final measures of the program's success:

- *Retention of key personnel:* How many of the original roster of LDP participants are still with the company?
- *Readiness of participants for higher-level positions:* How many of the original roster of LDP participants have been promoted or are ready for promotion? Also, how many promotional errors were avoided by being able to test this group of Hi-Pos *before* promoting them?
- *Application of learning to participants' current jobs:* Have the participants been able to transfer their learning throughout the program to improve their performance in their current jobs?
- *Problems solved and challenges overcome:* What problems have been solved and challenges overcome through the action-learning projects that would otherwise have continued to be unresolved?

Do You Want to Do It Again?

Of course, the ultimate judgment on the success or failure of your LDP will be determined by company executives' answer to this one question: *Do we want to run the program again for another group of Hi-Pos?*

There are several possible answers to this question:

- Yes, let's get another group started as soon as possible.
- Let's look at starting a lower-level LDP for a less experienced group of employees, or college hires, to accelerate their growth over time.
- Let's wait to see how well the graduates of this first program perform in higher-level roles before deciding to do this again.
- No, the program didn't meet expectations.

The executives' answer will depend on the success of this first program, on how great the demand is for new leadership, by the size of the company, and by the resources available. In a smaller company, it may be necessary to run the program only every few years, while a larger company may require a new cohort of Hi-Pos every year to meet the demands caused by retirement of baby boomers and the company's projected growth.

Summary

This chapter discussed how to get started with your LDP, including the selection of locations and faculty for the first LDP education session, the commitments you should ask LDP participants to make, and how to involve company executives in the program. How to bring closure to the LDP was also discussed, along with how to celebrate the program's conclusion. The ultimate evaluation measure for the LDP is whether company executives felt that the benefits of the program were sufficient to repeat the program with another group of Hi-Pos.

In the last chapter, we will discuss how much it will cost to run your LDP and discuss higher- and lower-cost alternatives.

Chapter 10

How Much Will It Cost?

═══════
What's In This Chapter

- What are some lower-cost and higher-cost alternatives for different types of expenses for LDP components?
- What is the LDP going to cost the company?
- What will it cost the company if you don't develop your next generation of leaders?
═══════

F ew small to mid-sized companies have the resources to build a leadership development facility like GE's Crotonville or to build a large leadership development staff. The LDP presented in this book requires neither type of investment. Yet, there are certainly substantial costs associated with running an LDP, and these fall into the following categories:

- faculty costs
- facility costs
- travel costs
- IT costs
- other costs.

This chapter will examine each category of costs, discuss higher- and lower-budget alternatives, and then calculate overall costs and cost per participant. Finally, this chapter will go on to examine the costs of *not* developing your company's next generation of leaders.

Faculty Costs

If you want to hire some of the biggest names in the leadership development field as faculty, you need to be prepared to pay their prices. Some of these gurus get $20,000 to $50,000 for a single speech or a single day of their time. As discussed in chapter 3, there are many business school faculty, consultants, and training vendors who work for much lower fees and can be just as effective in conducting your LDP education sessions. For example, you can use junior faculty (adjunct faculty or assistant professors) from leading business schools who are just as sharp and effective as their better-known, more senior colleagues; have experience teaching in their schools' executive education programs; and charge much lower fees, typically $2,000 to $5,000 per day.

While most business schools have an executive education department or director who will be happy to plan your entire LDP for you using the school's faculty, you will save a lot of money by going directly to the school's faculty members. Most business schools allow their faculty a specified number of days to do private consulting and education programs to supplement their salaries. This is not to imply that the business schools' executive education wouldn't do a great job for you, but only that you are going to pay for their overhead and their profit margin and will end up paying two to three times what you would pay if you hired a faculty member directly.

You should also feel free to try to negotiate a better price from any vendor. For example, a well-known business school professor (who had not yet reached "guru" status) quoted his fee as $7,500 per day. When told that the budget for the session was $12,000 for the 2.5-day session, he replied "I can work with that."

You can also negotiate with training vendors. If they want your business, they may be flexible on their charges. Many training vendors do not have their own trainers as full-time staff, but use contract trainers whom they have certified to give their programs. In these cases, you may get a better price for the program by finding one of the certified trainers and negotiating with that person directly, rather than going to the vendor. In many cases, the vendor's certified trainers are allowed to develop their own business, paying a per-participant fee to the vendor. If you go to the training vendor directly, you will be paying its overhead and profit margin and the trainer will get only a small percentage of the overall fee. As a result, you can often get a better price by purchasing the program from the certified trainer rather than directly from the training vendor.

The other alternative with training vendors is to license their program and have it presented by a member of your internal training staff. This will typically require your trainer to attend a certification program offered by the vendor. But, once certified, the only cost to the company of giving the program is a per-participant charge for training materials.

Teach Coaching Skills

I once needed to train several hundred managers in my company on coaching skills. I found a good two-day program from a vendor and paid $4,000 to attend its training/licensing program. Once I was licensed to give this program, my only obligation to the vendor was to buy participant notebooks from them at a cost of $150 each. The calculations of the savings to the company from this approach are given in figure 10-1.

Figure 10-1. Example of the cost of a licensed training.

Cost of the training/licensing program	$4,000
Cost for participant training notebooks ($150 × 200 participants)	$30,000
Total cost for 200 participants	$34,000
Cost per participant (34,000/200)	$170

If we had sent these 200 participants to a local university program on coaching skills, the cost would have averaged $795 per participant or $159,000. By licensing the program, we saved $125,000.

Some training vendors have a large catalog of half-day to three-day trainings on a wide variety of management and leadership topics and require only that your trainer take a facilitation skills course from them to be certified on the full catalog of programs (of course, there is also a materials fee for each participant for each program given).

You can also inquire of your company's executives what consultants they may already be using in the business. Your CEO or another executive may already have a consultant on retainer who would make an excellent instructor for one of your LDP education sessions, perhaps in partnership with that executive. Sometimes an executive who is using such a consultant can be very interested in getting the LDP participants educated on the consultant's approach or methodology and welcomes the opportunity to get this group of Hi-Pos thinking along the same lines.

Of course, you should follow the guidelines in chapter 3 around selecting faculty, whether they are business school faculty, consultants, training providers, or internal trainers.

Facility Costs

Where are you going to hold your LDP education sessions, and how much will it cost to house and feed the participants? Selection of facilities for your education sessions was discussed briefly in chapter 9. Typically, you will want to hold your first session near your company's headquarters to facilitate the participation of company executives. Other sessions may be held near other company facilities, including foreign headquarters. While it would be nice if every company had a facility like GE's Crotonville center, few small and mid-sized companies have this capability. In choosing a facility, consider several alternatives:

- hotels
- conference centers
- universities
- supplier or customer facilities.

Hotels

Hotels are in the business of hosting these types of sessions. They love this type of business because it generates room revenue, meal revenue, and conference space revenue, and they will charge you for anything and everything you use. Some hotels have better conference facilities than others—you probably want to avoid being in a partitioned section of a large ballroom with paper-thin wall dividers while other sections are being used simultaneously by other groups. If your company's marketing department has a meeting planner on staff, ask to use the planner's services—meeting planners typically know local facilities and are comfortable negotiating with the hotels' sales staffs. If your company does not have a meeting planner on staff, you might consider finding one who works in the geographical area in which you want to hold the education session.

In negotiating with a hotel's sales staff, realize that they want to make a sale and can be flexible. At a minimum, given that you will have participants staying in hotel rooms for the duration of the program and that you will be feeding everyone several times a day, you should be able to get the hotel to waive charges for using its conference space. Many hotels will have conference packages that include sumptuous meals, extravagant coffee breaks, and snacks available throughout the day. Consider what you need to provide to the participants to keep them comfortable, but don't plan elaborate lunches unless you want them to fall asleep during your afternoon session. Look at your company's culture and business guidelines. Do you want to provide an open bar before dinner, put wine on the dinner tables, offer a cash bar, or let participants pay for their own beverages at the hotel bar? Tell the hotel exactly what you want, and ask them to give you a price.

Also, look at the hotel's conference facilities and what they include. If they have LCD projectors built into each conference room that are included in their fees, you can save yourself $400 to $600 per day to rent a projector. If they do not include projectors and screens in the room fees, ask if you can bring your own to save these fees. Similarly, if you need to use flip charts, hotels will often charge $25 to $60 per day per

165

easel—it may be less costly for you to purchase a few portable easels and carry them to your education sessions. Similarly, does the hotel provide wireless personal computer network connections for participants, and is this included in the room fee? If not, some hotels charge $10 to $15 per room per night for these connections, and these charges can add up to a substantial sum over the course of a three-day program.

Conference Centers

In or near almost every large city in the world, you will find conference centers that provide all of the services you will find at a hotel. More important, the conference centers typically will cost less per participant than a major hotel and will have better meeting facilities. A conference center will often provide a more relaxed atmosphere than a major city hotel; have better facilities for meetings and break-out sessions (if required for your education program); and will include LCD projectors, flip charts, and other audiovisual equipment in their base-level fees. They may also have such amenities as beverage stations where participants can get coffee or soft drinks at any time of day (without paying large extra fees) and free wireless network connections.

As with the discussion of hotel costs, consider all costs negotiable—if the package plan offered by the conference center seems too extravagant and costly for your needs, tell them exactly what you want and ask them for a price.

Universities

Many universities have their own excellent conference facilities that offer very competitive rates compared to local hotels and private conference centers. These university-based centers are typically a separate business from the university itself, that is, you don't have to hire a university professor to teach your education session to rent the conference facilities. Even some smaller colleges have established continuing education centers, in or near major cities, that they primarily use in the evenings or on weekends and would be very happy to rent them to your company for a relatively small fee. They can also recommend local caterers.

Universities can be even more flexible if you are running an education session during the summer. One LDP held a summer session at Cambridge University in the United Kingdom. Participants stayed in dormitory rooms, and while these were certainly not on par with first-class hotel rooms, just being at such a prestigious university and having excellent catering (with a dinner in a dining room that was built in the 16th century) made it an outstanding experience.

Customer/Supplier Facilities

While your company may not have a leadership development center, perhaps one of your customers or suppliers has such a center that they would allow you (for free or for a small fee) to use for one or more of your LDP education sessions. You will never know unless you ask.

Travel Costs

Unless your company is totally based in one location (more and more unlikely in today's global economy), you are going to have to incur travel and related expenses to bring all of your Hi-Pos together for your LDP education sessions. While there is a tendency to want to hold all education sessions near the company headquarters location to minimize time and travel requirements for company executives, holding sessions near a variety of company locations can help LDP participants better understand the scope of the company's business and get a wider range of company executives involved in the program.

One decision you will have to make is whether to have participants charge their travel expenses to their local cost centers or to pay the expenses from a centralized corporate budget. On the one hand, it can be argued that because you are developing the company's future leaders, the expenses should come from a central budget; on the other hand, it can also be argued that the LDP is also intended to improve the performance of the participants in their current jobs, so the expenses should come from their local budgets. There is no one correct answer, so this deserves some discussion with corporate executives.

If you have a corporate travel department or a corporate travel agency, talk with the people in that department about negotiating reduced airfares for your LDP sessions. While this is more difficult to do than in decades past, it is still possible with some airlines. Encourage LDP participants to plan other local meetings around the LDP schedule so as to minimize extra travel costs.

Information Technology Costs

Because all LDP participants are Hi-Pos, you can assume that they will want to continue to do their regular jobs while attending the LDP education sessions. Hopefully, you will schedule these sessions at a hotel or other conference facility that provides free network connectivity. Even if this is the case, ask your IT department to ensure that using the facility's wireless network will not pose any problems in penetrating your company's firewall. You may also want to ask your IT department to set up several computers for use by those participants who do not have laptops or notebook computers to bring to the sessions.

There may also be instances where you require additional support from your IT department. For example, an education session may require that all participants have networked computers, such as to run a business simulation. Or all participants may need Internet connectivity to access materials needed for an education session, such as to do competitive research for a session that focuses on strategic marketing. In some cases, the education vendor may be able to provide all of the equipment that is needed along with technical support on-site (of course, you will need to pay for this). In other cases, your IT department may need to take responsibility for setting up and supporting the equipment.

In any of these cases, your IT department should do this out of its own budget.

Other Costs

While many of the tasks listed for the HR group, training group, IT group, and company executives can be seen as part of their regular jobs, it is strongly recommended that a member of the company's HR or training group be designated as the LDP manager, and this can add a headcount to the company's staffing.

If you do not have a meeting planner within the company, you may want to contract with a meeting planning professional to help negotiate facilities contracts and handle logistical arrangements.

If your company has no experience with leadership development, you may also want to hire an external consultant to advise the LDP manager on program structure, identify instructional resources, and provide general support for the program and the LDP manager.

There will certainly be other expenses associated with your LDP. Some will be necessary, and some will be optional. Some of these added expenses include the following:

- If you are holding an education session near one of your major manufacturing plants, you may want to include a tour of the plant for the participants and you may need to hire buses to get them there.
- If you choose some of the optional features of the LDP, such as assigning books or articles for participants to read, you will need a budget for purchasing those books or reprints of the required articles.
- To help group cohesiveness, you may want to create special baseball caps or coffee cups or portfolios for the participants. You might ask your marketing communications group to create a special logo for the LDP and use the logo on whatever item you choose to give the participants. These can become treasured items as explained in the sidebar.
- If your company does not already have a contract with a web conferencing company, you may incur expenses to hold the virtual follow-up sessions.

Earning Your LDP Baseball Cap

In one LDP I ran, we decided to purchase baseball caps for the participants, each with a special logo we created for the LDP. When we handed these out at the second LDP education session, they were well received.

As I handed them to the participants, I also gave one to my boss, the senior vice president of HR. She asked if she could also have one for the company CEO.

The CEO had not attended either the first or the second LDP session, and this was a very clear bone of contention with the participants. Rather than just give her a hat for the CEO, I asked the participants whether we should provide a cap for the CEO. The response was overwhelming: "Give it to him when he shows up—he's got to earn it!"

When the CEO attended the third education session and spent several hours talking with the participants, I then asked the participants whether we should give him a hat. There was an acclamation that he had now "earned his hat." The incident may seem very minor, but it did much to improve the cohesiveness of the LDP group, and the message was not lost on the CEO.

If your company's LDP is successful, you may want to end the program with some type of celebration. For example, you might want to hold a formal dinner with the CEO and other executives in attendance and award a certificate or plaque to each participant. If your budget permits, you might consider inviting spouses to this ceremony or to hire a well-known guru to speak at the dinner. With or without the budget for this, the group should be addressed by the CEO or by the board chairman.

Bottom-Line Cost of Running an LDP

The suggested LDP model includes eight quarterly sessions over a two-year period. Table 10-1 lists estimated variable costs for groups of 25, 36, and 50 participants. Along with the variable costs will be the cost of the LDP manager (a full-time position) and the time and effort required of other company employees (e.g., HR and training staff, executives, IT staff) to make your LDP a success. The table also excludes the costs of participant travel.

For an LDP with 36 participants, use a guideline of $15,000 per session for faculty and related educational expenses and $15,000 per session for facilities, meals, and other expenses. For a two-year LDP encompassing eight education sessions, this is a total program budget of $240,000, or

Table 10-1. Variable costs for each LDP education session.

Cost Category	25 Participants	36 Participants	50 Participants
Faculty	$5,000–$15,000	$5,000–$15,000	$5,000–$15,000
Facilities, Meals, and Miscellaneous	$10,000–$15,000	$14,000–$20,000	$20,000–$30,000
Total Variable Costs (per session)	$15,000–$30,000	$19,000–$35,000	$25,000–$45,000
Average Cost per Participant	$600–$1,200	$528–$972	$500–$900

$6,667 per person. Compare this with the cost of a leadership development seminar at leading business schools or other well-known training providers, which can range from $6,000 to $15,000 or more for a one-week program that will provide neither the breadth of subject matter nor the opportunities to apply learning through action-learning projects, and are focused on a generic audience, rather than being tailored to your company's and your participants' specific requirements.

Costs of *Not* Preparing Your Next Generation of Leaders

Compare the cost of creating your LDP to the cost of *not* preparing your company's next generation of leaders:

- How many of your company's executives are eligible for retirement in the next five to 10 years? How are you going to replace them all and ensure continuity in company leadership? *Creating your own LDP helps to build your leadership pipeline so that you have capable successors ready to replace those who retire.*
- What does it cost to recruit a senior executive from outside the company? Besides an executive search that can cost you up to one-third of the new executive's first-year's salary, what is the cost to the business of having the position vacant for the time it takes to conduct the search, get someone on board, and then get the new person up to speed? *Building your own LDP helps to prepare*

successors from within the company who are already steeped in the company culture, already know the company's business, and have already developed their own networks and working relationships within the company.

- What does it cost the company to promote someone to a senior position who fails in that position? Consider not just the cost to the bottom line, but also what it does to employee morale to see someone promoted and subsequently fired. *Through your LDP, you not only prepare Hi-Pos for future leadership positions, but also get to test their capabilities before promoting them.*

- What does it cost the company to have a high level of turnover among your Hi-Pos who see that the company isn't willing to invest in their future with the company and that company executives often look outside the company to fill vacancies, rather than promote from within? *When employees see that the company is investing in their future, they are much more likely to stay with the company.*

The basic question is *not* "Should the company invest in an LDP?" but rather, "Can the company afford *not* to invest in developing its next generation of leaders?"

This book has been written to help small and mid-sized companies plan and run their own LDPs, and the time to start is now!

Appendix

Potential Topics for Your LDP Education Sessions

There are dozens of topics you could choose for LDP education sessions, and for each topic, there are many variations and approaches to the topic that will depend on the faculty you choose for a particular session.

Here are 12 topics that you might consider. Each brief topic description has been extracted from the offerings of business school executive education programs and seminars offered by a variety of training vendors. These are not meant to be complete descriptions, but only brief overviews of what might be included in each education session along with an idea or two about the type of action-learning projects you might assign to your LDP participants to follow on from the education session.

Don't limit yourself to this list. As explained throughout the book, you should select topics that match your company's key competencies and the needs of your LDP participants.

1. Stepping Up to Leadership
2. Leading Change and Organizational Renewal
3. Fundamentals of Finance for Non-Financial Executives
4. Understanding and Solving Complex Business Problems
5. Reengineering Business Processes
6. Customer-Focused Innovation

7. Reinventing Your Business Strategy
8. Negotiations and Decision-Making Strategies
9. Leading Successful Change
10. Achieving Outstanding Performance
11. Getting Results Without Authority
12. Leading Virtual and Remote Teams.

Stepping Up to Leadership

This session, or something similar to it, is recommended for your first LDP education session.

Session Content

- Defining what it means to be a leader
- Assessing personal leadership traits and debriefing on results
- Identifying leadership strengths and areas needing development
- Determining what derails leaders
- Discussing alternate career paths
  —Management/Leadership career track
  —Technical career track
- Achieving work–life balance
- Writing a personal vision statement.

Action-Learning Assignment

- Assign each LDP participant to write a personal vision statement and review it with team members.
- Have the LDP participants present their personal vision statements to a panel of company executives at the start of the next LDP education session.

Leading Change and Organizational Renewal

Leading change is a vital skill for leaders, and one of your LDP education sessions should cover this.

Session Content

- Conducting a SWOT (strengths, weaknesses, opportunities, and threats) analysis of your organization
- Assessing and managing organizational culture, identifying problem areas, and implementing change
- Building a shared vocabulary around cultural and change issues
- Building your vision of the future and selling it to your company's internal and external stakeholders.

Action-Learning Assignment

- Conduct a SWOT analysis on an assigned organization or group within the company.
- Develop and implement an assigned change strategy.

Fundamentals of Finance for Non-Financial Executives

Leading a company requires that individuals have a firm grasp of the company's financial situation. This education session will provide basic terminology and skills for those LDP participants who have never taken a corporate finance course.

Session Content

- Understanding basic accounting and finance principles and vocabulary
- Learning to read and analyze company financial statements
- Learning common financial measurements and how to calculate them
- Understanding the dynamics of how your company makes and spends money
- Understanding how to build a budget.

Action-Learning Assignment

- Assign individuals or teams of LDP participants to analyze the financial statements and key productivity measures of your company, its primary competitors, and similar companies in your industry.

- Assign individual LDP participants to work on due diligence teams that are considering a company acquisition.

Understanding and Solving Complex Business Problems

As individuals rise higher in a company's hierarchy, the problems they will face become more complex. Participants need to develop their own understanding and methods of solving complex business problems.

Session Content

- Using systems thinking to analyze complex business processes
- Articulating problems
- Defining structural problems versus behavioral problems
- Diagnosing causes of complex business problems
- Thinking systematically to solve complex problems
- Generating and evaluating alternate solutions.

Action-Learning Assignment

- Assign teams of LDP participants long-standing business problems to analyze, recommend solutions, and test those solutions.
- Ask individual LDP participants to apply these new methods to problems they are facing in their regular jobs and to report back on the results.

Reengineering Business Processes

Business process reengineering is a valuable methodology that has received a poor reputation because many companies have used it as an excuse for massive layoffs without ever actually doing the required analysis.

Session Content

- Discussing fundamentals of business process reengineering
- Creating a process map

- Analyzing business processes
- Planning solutions
- Implementing solutions
- Assessing results.

Action-Learning Assignment

- Assign teams of LDP participants to analyze a business process outside their own domains and make recommendations for improving those processes.
- Ask individual LDP participants to use the reengineering process to improve the workings of their own groups (requires cooperation of their managers).

Customer-Focused Innovation

Creativity and innovation are important topics for company leaders, and adding the focus on customers can make this an outstanding session.

Session Content

- Understanding customer needs—a systematic approach
- Describing principles of rapid prototyping
- Overcoming bureaucratic resistance to innovation and change
- Assessing the benefits of becoming customer-centric.

Action-Learning Assignment

- Assign teams of LDP participants to undertake a project using this methodology.
- Define the parameters of the projects, or let the participants do this themselves.

Reinventing Your Business Strategy

This topic focuses on the creation of business strategy. It should be placed toward the end of the LDP agenda.

Session Content

- Defining the importance of reinventing your business strategy
- Describing the basics of strategy development
- Understanding critical analysis of current strategies
- Focusing on the voice of the customer
- Building a new business strategy
- Selling your new strategy.

Action-Learning Assignment

- Assign teams of LDP participants to use the methodology they learned in this session to analyze an assigned business strategy and make recommendations to reinvent that strategy.
- Assign teams of LDP participants to work with the executives in their own business units, functions, or geographical areas on reviewing their strategies.

Negotiations and Decision-Making Strategies

The higher people rise in an organization, the tougher the decisions they must make. This session will give them the tools and skills to better handle negotiations and complex decision making.

Session Content

- Understanding the psychology of judgment and decision making
- Discussing organizational decision making
- Describing influence techniques
- Understanding problem solving
- Creating value
- Defining action planning.

Action-Learning Assignment

- Instruct LDP participants to use the techniques learned in a negotiation situation that arises in their regular jobs and to report back on the results.

Leading Successful Change

An earlier session suggestion in this appendix dealt with leading change and organizational renewal, focusing on performing SWOT analyses, and managing organizational culture. The focus of this session is more on leading people through a major change, and it should be in one of the later LDP education sessions.

Session Content

- Helping others see the need for change
- Inspiring and influencing people to change
- Overcoming obstacles to change
- Creating and sustaining momentum
- Assessing your change leadership skills.

Action-Learning Assignment

- Ask LDP participants to work with company executives to facilitate a major change effort sponsored by those senior executives.
- Have the LDP participants share their results and experiences at the next LDP education session.

Achieving Outstanding Performance

Performance management is always a hot topic, dealing with how to get the best performance from your company's people and its business operations.

Session Content

- Identifying which business processes are key to creating value
- Calculating the costs and benefits of key activities and processes
- Unleashing the forces of commitment, innovation, and engagement in your employees
- Building outstanding performance and then sustaining it.

Action-Learning Assignment

- Assign individual LDP participants to select an appropriate project that is in the scope of their current job responsibilities.

- Apply the methodologies learned in this session to work on projects assigned by company executives to make recommendations to improve performance of underperforming parts of the company's business.

Getting Results Without Authority

Influencing and negotiating skills are important at all levels of the organization, and they will prove valuable to LDP participants whether or not they are eventually promoted.

Session Content
- Building credibility (a prerequisite to influencing)
- Understanding others and adapting your influencing style based on that understanding
- Developing your influencing and negotiating skills
- Developing and growing relationships
- Creating a collaborative work environment.

Action-Learning Assignment
- Assign LDP participants to practice the methodologies learned in this session.
- Have LDP participants report back on two or more situations where they applied their learning to their current jobs.

Leading Virtual and Remote Teams

In today's global business environment, managers and leaders at all levels often find that they are managing and leading people who are not their direct reports or who are not collocated with the rest of their teams. This session will prove valuable to everyone who is in this situation.

Session Content
- Defining the differences between virtual, remote, and face-to-face teams
- Identifying common problems facing virtual and remote teams

- Developing, planning, and communicating strategies to overcome identified problems
- Describing online tools that can be used to make virtual and remote teams more effective.

Action-Learning Assignment

- Assign team membership to ensure that teams are spread over substantial distances.
- Define projects for those teams, requiring that the teams use the methodologies learned in this session to accomplish those projects.

References

Badaway, Michael. 1995. *Developing Managerial Skills in Engineers and Scientists: Succeeding as a Technical Manager*, 2d ed. New York: Van Nostrand Reinhold.

Betof, Edward. 2009. *Leaders as Teachers.* Alexandria, VA: ASTD Press.

Bossidy, Larry, Ram Charan, and Charles Burke. 2002. *Execution: The Discipline of Getting Things Done.* New York: Crown Business.

Clinton, Hillary Rodham. 2006. *It Takes a Village*, 10th ed. New York: Simon & Schuster.

Dobson, Michael, and Susan Wilson. 2008. *Goal Setting: How to Create an Action Plan and Achieve Your Goals.* New York: AMACOM.

Drucker, Peter F. 1993. *Post-Capitalist Society.* New York: HarperBusiness.

Goldsmith, Marshall, and Mark Reiter. 2007. *What Got You Here Won't Get You There.* New York: Hyperion Books.

Kirkpatrick, Donald, and James Kirkpatrick. 2006. *Evaluating Training Programs: The Four Levels*, 3rd ed. San Francisco: Berrett-Koehler.

Martin, Chuck, Peg Martin, and Richard Guare. 2007. *Smarts: Are We Hard-Wired for Success?* New York: AMACOM.

Tiku, Nitasha. 2007. "Boomer Benefits." *Inc.*, August 1, www.inc.com/magazine/20070801/boomer-benefits.html.

Tobin, Daniel R. 1997. *The Knowledge Enabled Organization: Moving from Training to Learning to Meet Business Goals.* New York: AMACOM.

Tobin, Daniel R., and Margaret S. Pettingell. 2008. *The AMA Guide to Management Development.* New York: AMACOM.

Ulrich, David, Steven Kerr, and Ron Ashkenas. 2002. *The GE Work-Out: How to Implement GE's Revolutionary Method for Busting Bureaucracy & Attacking Organizational Problems.* New York: McGraw-Hill.

About the Author

Daniel Tobin is a consultant, coach, and author on corporate learning strategies and leadership development programs. He has worked in the training and development field for 30 years, including four years as vice president of design and development at the American Management Association, 11 years at Digital Equipment Corporation where he founded Digital's Network University, and two years at Wang Global/Getronics where he founded Wang Global/Getronics Virtual University. Tobin has extensive experience in leadership and management development, executive education, sales and sales support training, and technical education. He has taught courses on leadership, effective teamwork, organizational transformation, and coaching skills, and he has given workshops and keynotes to executives, human resources groups, and training organizations on five continents. He has also acted as a coach to corporate training directors on how to align their learning initiatives more closely with their companies' business goals and strategies and to human resources and training groups on how to build leadership development programs, using the model described in this book.

Tobin is the author of five books on corporate learning strategies:

- *The AMA Guide to Management Development* (with Margaret Pettingell; AMACOM, 2008)
- *All Learning Is Self-Directed: How Organizations Can Encourage and Support Independent Learning* (ASTD, 2000)
- *The Knowledge-Enabled Organization: Moving from Training to Learning to Meet Business Goals* (AMACOM, 1997)

- *Transformational Learning: Renewing Your Company Through Knowledge and Skills* (Wiley, 1996)
- *Re-Educating the Corporation: Foundations for the Learning Organization* (Wiley, 1994).

Tobin's articles and press interviews have appeared in leading business and professional publications around the world. Noted for his practical approaches and his sense of humor, he is a popular speaker and seminar/workshop leader.

Tobin earned a master's degree from the Johnson Graduate School of Management and a PhD in the economics of education, both from Cornell University. He was included in *Leadership Excellence* magazine's 2008–9 Top 100 list of thought leaders on leadership. To see what others have said about Tobin, please refer to his profile and recommendations on LinkedIn at www.linkedin.com/in/danieltobin.

If you have any questions about the material presented in this book, please let Tobin know by visiting his website at www.tobincls.com or emailing him at danieltobin@att.net.

THE ASTD MISSION:

Through exceptional learning and performance, we create a world that works better.

The American Society for Training & Development provides world-class professional development opportunities, content, networking, and resources for workplace learning and performance professionals.

Dedicated to helping members increase their relevance, enhance their skills, and align learning to business results, ASTD sets the standard for best practices within the profession.

The society is recognized for shaping global discussions on workforce development and providing the tools to demonstrate the impact of learning on the organizational bottom line. ASTD represents the profession's interests to corporate executives, policy makers, academic leaders, small business owners, and consultants through world-class content, convening opportunities, professional development, and awards and recognition.

Resources
- *T+D (Training + Development)* Magazine
- ASTD Press
- Industry Newsletters
- Research and Benchmarking
- Representation to Policy Makers

Networking
- Local Chapters
- Online Communities
- ASTD Connect
- Benchmarking Forum
- Learning Executives Network

Professional Development
- Certificate Programs
- Conferences and Workshops
- Online Learning
- CPLP™ Certification Through the ASTD Certification Institute
- Career Center and Job Bank

Awards and Best Practices
- ASTD BEST Awards
- Excellence in Practice Awards
- E-Learning Courseware Certification (ECC) Through the ASTD Certification Institute

Learn more about ASTD at www.astd.org.
1.800.628.2783 (U.S.) or 1.703.683.8100
customercare@astd.org

080615.31410

About Berrett-Koehler Publishers

Berrett-Koehler is an independent publisher dedicated to an ambitious mission: Creating a World That Works for All.

We believe that to truly create a better world, action is needed at all levels—individual, organizational, and societal. At the individual level, our publications help people align their lives with their values and with their aspirations for a better world. At the organizational level, our publications promote progressive leadership and management practices, socially responsible approaches to business, and humane and effective organizations. At the societal level, our publications advance social and economic justice, shared prosperity, sustainability, and new solutions to national and global issues.

Visit our website

Go to www.bkconnection.com to read exclusive excerpts of new books, get special discounts, see videos of our authors, read their blogs, find out about author appearances and other BK events, browse our complete catalog, and more!

Get the *BK Communiqué,* our free eNewsletter

News about Berrett-Koehler, yes—new book announcements, special offers, author interviews. But also news by Berrett-Koehler authors, employees, and fellow travelers. Tales of the book trade. Links to our favorite websites and videos—informative, amusing, sometimes inexplicable. Trivia questions—win a free book! Letters to the editor. And much more!

See a sample issue: www.bkconnection.com/BKCommunique.

BK® Berrett–Koehler Publishers, Inc.
San Francisco. *www.bkconnection.com*

Index